LANGUAGE TEACHING IN KINDERGARTEN AND THE EARLY PRIMARY GRADES

Language Teaching

IN KINDERGARTEN AND THE EARLY PRIMARY GRADES

by

Mildred A. Dawson

Sacramento State College

and

Georgiana Collis Newman

Los Angeles City Schools

HARCOURT, BRACE & WORLD, INC.

New York · Chicago · Burlingame

LANGUAGE TEACHING IN KINDERGARTEN AND THE EARLY PRIMARY GRADES
is a revision of LANGUAGE TEACHING IN GRADES 1 AND 2
by Mildred A. Dawson.

Contents

LANGUAGE TEACHING IN KINDERGARTEN AND THE EARLY PRIMARY GRADES

A cheerful, spacious, and stimulating room, with adequate provision for small-group activity, encourages adjustment and learning in the early school years.

Flint Community Schools, Flint, Michigan

1

The Language Arts Program and the Child

IN RECENT years major investigations like those of Loban (p. 25) and Strickland (p. 26) have revealed the true story of children's language development, including its variability. The studies show that English-speaking school beginners have developed a mastery of the basic patterns of English, regardless of native ability or environmental influences (except for genuinely subnormal children), but differ greatly in conceptual background, size and nature of vocabulary, length and vividness of sentences, and ability and willingness to participate freely in oral language situations. While sex and intelligence are important in the development of language, socio-economic influences are of crucial significance. Children who enter school using standard English and enjoying a rich background of experiences are shown to have a distinct advantage over those having a meager background and speaking in dialects quite different from standard English; the advantage is especially marked in respect to readiness and ease in learning to read.

Dealing with children who are accustomed to hearing and using dialects unlike the standard English spoken by the teacher and found in school books is a difficult problem. Neither research nor accepted practice has yet shown the procedures most effective in making these children feel secure and willing to talk freely while they are growing accustomed to standard English. While this book does present the issue and suggests some practicable ways of dealing with it, final solutions await further investigations and experimental teaching.

Probably the most important of the factors that determine the general nature of the kindergarten-primary language arts program are the characteristics of growing children, the influence of the social environment in which they develop, and the nature of the modern school curriculum with its governing purposes and interrelationships. This chapter will discuss in considerable detail the influences these factors have on the language curriculum in the early school years.

Children in the Early School Years

A school beginner speaks the language which is used in his home. If his parents use a reasonably literate type of English, if they customarily talk over plans and happenings with him, if he is a part of the family conversations and discussions, he is likely to be fluent and responsive in school. On the other hand, if his parents do not use literate English, if they seldom carry on family discussions or easy, flowing conversations, if he receives and hears only curt commands—possibly expressed crudely or illiterately—he may have little to contribute at school, he will be unaccustomed to planning and discussion sessions, and he may feel uncomfortable in his inability to speak standard English.

Recent investigations have indicated that children with the most meager language development come from homes with some or all of the following situations: (1) Behavior problems and family situations are rarely talked over. Instead, a child may be told, "Shut up" or "Get out of here," or be given some other curt order. (2) The family does few things together—seldom takes trips or makes visits to the zoo or park or library, for instance. There is little to talk about, and little is said. Thus, the child lacks language experience. (3) Both parents may work, and the child has little contact with adults in the family.

A lesser disadvantage may come from the use of a dialect with terms not used at school; for instance, *poke* for *bag, tote* for *carry, fixing to* for *planning to, hap* for *bed cover,* terms the author found to be commonly used in one community. The teacher should accept without comment these localized and interesting terms and do everything possible to extend experiences and to provide the vocabulary for talking about them, to read and tell stories that introduce words which the child may absorb and later use through unconscious imitation. School-age children still acquire language imitatively, and the teacher can provide the model that will extend language beyond the customary, localized, dialectal terminology.

In general, we can expect a child to enter kindergarten or first grade with a considerable background in language. He is likely to have learned to listen comprehensively to directions and explanations as well as to stories, discussion, and conversation. At the same time, he will have developed some ability to express himself in these same ways. He typically will have acquired a fairly large vocabulary which he can organize into meaningful sentences in all basic patterns. Most of the words he speaks will be articulated with reasonable correctness and clarity as he relates an experience, poses questions, gives directions to a companion, engages in dramatic play, repeats a favorite rhyme, or tells a story.

PRESCHOOL VOCABULARY AND LANGUAGE ABILITY

It is probable that the average six-year-old has a speaking vocabulary somewhat in excess of 2500 words and that his meaning (or listening) vocabulary may be as large as 17,000 basic words and 7000 derivatives; a five-year-old's vocabulary would be correspondingly extensive, but smaller. Sentences, spoken according to the patterns of the adult language he has heard, will average five or six words in length with some being quite long. So extensive a growth in language during the preschool years reflects a wealth of concepts, interests, verbal skills, and thought-power that the teacher of a young child can tap and utilize in guiding him to greater skill in all the language arts.

As stated above, children of the same age vary widely in their language proficiency. Differences may be due to level of intelligence, degree of emotional s ability, relation to siblings in the family, sex, and comparative literacy and richness of the language used in the home. Retardation in language growth, then, may be due to (1) having unusually low intelligence, (2) being shy or reticent because of social inexperience or feelings of inadequacy and being unwanted at home, (3) being a twin or triplet who is closely associated with one or more children equally immature in the use of language, (4) being a boy (boys are typically slower to develop than girls of comparable intelligence), and (5) coming from a home in which experiences are barren and the language patterns of adults meager and illiterate.

Authorities in the language arts recommend that teachers of disadvantaged children in kindergarten and the early primary grades encourage the continued use of the children's home-learned dialect and that they direct their efforts to building new and broader concepts through school experiences that fill gaps in the children's home-based backgrounds. Particularly, the boys and girls should be encouraged to participate in discussion and conversation and thus to add to their meager vocabulary and to build feelings of belonging and being important in their group. To what extent and at what stage teachers of young children should aim to change boys' and girls' faulty speech are moot points. Researchers in language put two policies first: (1) have the child feel comfortable in using his customary speech patterns, and (2) concentrate on the constant extension and enrichment of experiences and related language activities. These experts believe that reduction or elimination of illiterate expressions is secondary and is more the task of the intermediate-grade than of the primary-grade teacher. Actually, the language of disadvantaged young children is likely to improve in school even if teachers make no direct attack on illiteracies and errors. Boys and girls will tend to pick up the pronunciations, vocabulary, and intonations of their teacher, who is telling and reading stories, giving directions and explanations, and leading them in conversation and discussion. Liberal daily doses of literature—both verse and prose—contribute to language growth. Experienced teachers have also found that children who play the role of the teacher or some other typical user of standard English have a natural inclination to speak as these literate adults would and to shed temporarily their own illiterate expressions. Thus role-playing and dramatization may be used to accustom children's tongues to standard English without conscious effort or any self-consciousness on their part.

SOCIAL DEVELOPMENT

The kindergarten child is accustomed to associating with his family and with neighbors, most of whom are older or younger than he. Entering kindergarten may be a very strange experience indeed if, for the first time, he is one of thirty children of about the same age and size.

The child may feel lost in the crowd, especially if he finds none of his customary playmates there. The teacher's first responsibility is to help him feel at home, to give him a feeling of personal identity even as he is, at the same time, learning to subordinate any personal wishes that do not fit in with group decisions. Learning to take turns, to share, to cooperate, to contribute for the benefit of others are the social learnings to be attained.

What characteristics must the teacher consider in promoting the child's social learnings and development? First, the young child is interested in the *here* and the *now*. He wants something this minute, this morning, today, not a half-hour or a half-day later. To him, tomorrow may never come and yesterday is unimportant. The five- or six-year-old knows his home, his street, his shopping center, his classroom, and his playground; it is with these places that he is mainly concerned. As he progresses into the seven- and eight-year-old stages, he discovers an expanding environment and senses a lengthening time span. Learning activities now can involve the larger community and its workers who make his life safe and comfortable; he can plan more and more aptly for the morrow and for next week. He remembers more certainly and clearly the lessons in group living and behavior which yesterday brought.

Second, the young child is egocentric. With him it is the *big I* and *little you*. However, this nature-ordained characteristic is susceptible to change through wise training and normal group experiences. The young child learns to take turns and to share, to cooperate in group activities—especially those involving only a few children in some joint enterprise—and to be considerate of others. These characteristics he develops, not so much through direct instruction and correction as through actual living in social situations. A young child must have firsthand experience if he is to develop social insight and acquire desirable attitudes and social behavior.

Egocentrism is often reflected in his language. When he hears a statement such as "My kitty climbed to the top of a telephone pole," his response is usually not a question or remark about his friend's kitten, but rather a statement about his own pet; for example, "My dog likes to chase cats." However, in proceeding through kindergarten and first grade, a child tends to outgrow mere parallelism, to develop an ability

Children should be given numerous opportunities to observe closely. Careful examination of natural objects helps them to understand the world of nature and provides for language use as they later describe or recall what they have seen.

to meet the minds of his associates, and to respond directly to their comments. Such development is encouraged as the school promotes situations in which children in pairs and small groups engage in activities of mutual interest and work to a common goal, such as building a bookcase from crates.

INTELLECTUAL CHARACTERISTICS

The young child is typically a curious, active learner. The real world has so much that is strange and marvelous; there is so much he does not understand; there are so many questions he feels impelled to ask. He needs and wants to feel and to touch, to taste and to smell, to inspect closely. Sensory learning through manipulative activities is required if he is to attain understanding, to note the interrelatedness of ideas, to gain concepts that yield vocabulary, and to increase his powers of expression through language.

One of the developmental tasks of a young child is to learn to discriminate between fact and fancy. The world of fairies, elves, giants, and dragons may seem no more unreal to him than the actual world of escalators, magic-eyed doors that open on approach, tape recorders that reproduce his voice, streaking jet planes, and astronauts propelled into space. Older and more experienced persons can help him to understand that the fantasy of books and television is enjoyable make-believe; they can help him to learn something of the workings of the wonders in his real world. They can start with his immediate environment and gradually lead him outward intellectually from the places he actually sees to areas far away, from today to tomorrow and yesterday and then to the distant future and the faraway past.

Because of the young child's short attention span, the teacher must change activities frequently so that each one is comparatively brief. As maturation brings a lengthening attention span, the teacher provides opportunities to persist in the learning experiences for longer and longer periods. At the same time, the early need for firsthand, manipulative learning grows somewhat less, and the child can gain ideas in more vicarious ways through pictures, oral explanations, and reading.

The teacher capitalizes on the child's natural imitativeness by using a well-modulated and pleasing voice, by enunciating clearly, by introducing new words meaningfully, and by speaking the standard English the child is eventually to adopt. When a teacher is courteous, neat, poised, and friendly, that spirit and manner tend to be reflected in the behavior of the boy or girl.

The child in kindergarten and first grade tends to be somewhat impetuous and uncritical in his learning activities. He quickly draws his picture or writes his story, then assumes the attitude of "I've done my job. What next?" On the other hand, the second grader typically has passed the early, crude stages of learning and has become more self-critical. In fact, he is said to be in the "eraser stage" because he uses his eraser almost more than his pencil. What he is learning to do, he wants to do well.

PHYSICAL DEVELOPMENT

The child in kindergarten and the early primary grades is active and restless. Because the physiological needs of his growing body call for large body movements, he cannot sit still too long, and the school program should be such that he can move about as he learns. For instance, he may go to the reading chart to "frame" a phrase or he may act out a portion of what he has just read. Social-studies activities may call for construction, painting at the easel, or role-playing. Through manual activity he can learn much of the "new math" with its relationships and number values.

While the young child has rather good control of the larger muscles of his body, he still lacks the finer coordinations of the smaller muscles of his feet, hands, and eyes. Because of the lesser demand that manuscript writing makes on his coordination, he learns it rather than the cursive form that he may learn to use in later school years. In addition, he may still be in the process of gaining control over his vocal organs; for instance, *l, r, s, z, sh, th, br,* and *wh* sounds may not be mastered until the age of eight.

The Modern Curriculum

The planner of the language arts program must consider both the nature of the child and the social conditions in which he lives. The curriculum must provide for learnings in terms of the child's degree of maturation—his current interests and his basic ability to carry on learning activities at his present stage of development. Because the young child is so active a learner, who needs abundant firsthand experience, the program must provide much sensory learning, must involve him in social situations where he solves real problems in developing workable relations with his companions and in planning with them how to dramatize or how to portray in art his learnings about his community or the wider world. The modern curriculum may be considered an activity program that is socially centered; it is one in which the language arts are integrated among themselves and with all other aspects of the curriculum.

SCHEDULING LANGUAGE ACTIVITIES

Of the approximately 300 minutes in the school day, how many involve the use of language? Much of the time, someone will be speaking while others listen and possibly respond in kind. Less time will be given to writing. Even when members of the class are not actually communicating among themselves or with their teacher, they are likely to be engaged in learning activities that yield ideas and vocabulary. Throughout the entire day, in every lesson, there are constant opportunities for the use and enrichment of language.

Study of the following daily programs will show how listening, speaking, reading, or writing occur during the entire school day. In particular, note the blocks of time given to social studies and reading. Whether the teacher prefers standard grouping procedures or working more with individuals and short-term groups, opportunities for using language abound. The programs were submitted by expert primary teachers, one favoring social studies early in the day and the other starting with reading.

DAILY PROGRAM A

Before school	Individual interests
9:00– 9:20	Entire group activities: checking attendance, sharing news, miscellaneous routine matters
9:20–10:15	Social studies block (*time allotment flexible*)
	Planning activities 15 minutes
	Learning activities 25 minutes
	Evaluation; sharing; clean-up 15 minutes

10:15–10:30	Language activities (oral) related to the social studies: poems, stories, dramatization
10:30–10:55	Play and rest period
10:55–11:20	Reading: Group 1 (*seatwork and creative art*
11:20–11:45	Reading: Group 2 *for non-reading groups*)
12:45– 1:00	Story time
1:00– 1:25	Reading: Group 3 (*seatwork and art for others*)
1:25– 1:45	Writing: Copying a dictated announcement or note, creative stories dictated to teacher and later read from a chart, practice on manuscript writing
1:45– 2:00	Rest or play
2:00– 2:20	Number activities
2:20– 2:40	Music

DAILY PROGRAM B

Before school	Free period for individually chosen activities
9:00– 9:20	Show-and-tell period; routine matters
9:20–10:35	Language arts block: Reading (*directed and free; individualized or by groups as situation demands*)
10:35–10:55	Play and rest period
10:55–11:55	Social studies block (*flexible time allotment to planning, learning activities, sharing and evaluation, and clean-up*)
1:00– 1:50	Language arts block Story time 15 minutes Language 35 minutes (*original and reproduced stories growing out of story hour; dramatization; poems; writing, including dictation to teacher with occasional copying; practice on manuscript writing*)
1:50– 2:05	Rest or play
2:05– 2:20	Number activities
2:20– 2:40	Music

(NOTE: Art is included as an integral part of block activities.)

INTERRELATIONSHIPS AMONG THE LANGUAGE ARTS

Typically, the language arts work in pairs: speaking assumes that there will be listening; writing calls for someone to read what has been written. Oral reading which is purposeful is for the benefit of listeners. Such working relationships among the language arts are important aids

Spontaneous expression, coordination, sense of balance, and beauty are results of rhythm time. Children learn to listen, gain a basic appreciation of music, and acquire number concepts through this activity.

Pittsburgh Public School System

in acquiring skills common to reading, writing, speaking, and listening.

Other interrelationships are based on the elements common to the four aspects of the language arts. In the first place, words are a common denominator. The child thinks in *words;* he expresses his ideas in *words;* he gains vicarious experiences by listening to or reading *words.* They are his vehicle of thought, of expression, and of impression. No wonder that measures taken to improve vocabulary in one of the language arts are so likely to increase or refine vocabulary in each of the other language arts. For instance, Jamie was told by his teacher: "Now you *are* in a predicament, Jamie! What are you going to do about it?" (He had approached the characters in the spontaneous dramatization of a story in the wrong order and had finished up without involving three of them.) Jamie then resumed his action in the middle of the play so as to include all characters. In his first speech, he said, "I'm in a predicament. I want to learn to sing. Can you help me?" He had picked up a new word from his teacher and put it to immediate, appropriate use. If he writes his grandmother about the day's experiences it is highly likely that he will ask how to spell predicament.

A second common element is auditory discrimination. Hearing a word accurately is prerequisite to saying it correctly, and good pronunciation is basic to spelling the word properly later on. This ability to hear the likenesses and differences in similar words is basic to correct speech, to phonics in reading and to sounding and letter order in spelling. Listening, speaking, reading, writing—auditory discrimination underlies effectiveness in each of these four phases of the language arts.

RELATION TO OTHER CURRICULUM AREAS

Activities and lessons in the social studies field or in science have a dual role in promoting language instruction. The children's background is being enriched as they acquire new concepts and new vocabulary. In addition, the periods devoted to these content areas afford many opportunities for the children to communicate. They discuss plans and later report on their progress in carrying out their plans; they dramatize or tell stories; they give and take instructions; they make explanations; or they assist in listing duties, the names of committee members, and materials needed for carrying on an activity. There may also arise, within a social studies or science activity, a situation that calls for the planning, writing, and mailing of a letter.

In addition, social studies learnings may stimulate spontaneous expression during free conversation or free writing periods. The following conversation illustrates typical pupil reactions after a trip to the farm.

TERRY. What a good time we had at the farm yesterday!

MISS BOND. I'm glad you enjoyed the visit, Terry. Would all of you like to tell what you enjoyed most?

MAE. I liked the little chicks best. Two of them ate cornmeal from my hand.

PATTY. One of the chicks let me hold it. It was so soft and downy. I held my other hand over its back, and the chick went to sleep.

JACK. I like baby ducks better than little chicks. Baby ducks are so friendly. Did you see them come running up to me? I liked that. I picked one up and cuddled it. It was so soft!

BOBBY. Yes, I saw you. Do you know why they come running up to you? They want something to eat. I know, because I had some pet ducklings when I stayed on Uncle Dick's farm last summer. How they do gobble up their food!

KENNY. Do you know what I liked best? The lambs! How they did kick up their heels! They were so funny!

GEORGE. Funny! It was the little pigs that were funny. They put their noses through the fence and smelled my knees. Did you see the funny way their noses wiggled? When I reached down, they got scared and ran off. "Woof! Woof!" they went. I nearly died laughing at that funny old "Woof! Woof!"

SALLY. I liked all the animals we saw, but I liked the baby kittens best of all. Daddy is taking me back tomorrow. Mr. Black told me I could have one of the kittens for a pet.

This conversation was followed by a variety of activities which involved drawing pictures about the trip for the bulletin board and for a class booklet of stories, planning and developing a mural that depicted the arrival of the bus, with the animals assembled at the fence to watch, inviting parents to an exhibit and program of reports on the visit, and extensive reading of stories about farm animals. Many new concepts, numerous new words, and much experience in group conversation and discussion were outgrowths of this experience.

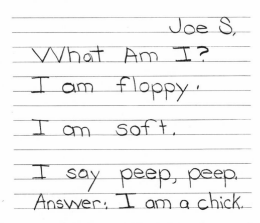

> Joe S,
> VVhat Am I?
> I am floppy.
>
> I am soft.
>
> I say peep, peep.
> Answer: I am a chick.

An original riddle by a second-grade child after the class saw chicks hatched in an incubator. Riddles encourage the use of descriptive words.

Major Aspects of the Language Arts Program

GROUP EXPRESSIONAL ACTIVITIES

At one period in the day, the girls and boys may relate personal experiences or observations in response to suggestions or questions from the teacher, who is seeking to develop a background for a story that is to be read. After the reading, the group may talk over episodes and characters in the story. At another period, they may discuss plans for an activity in the social studies program, such as setting up a classroom store patterned after the market or toy shop visited the day before, or writing a story summarizing their experiences on the trip. Other language situations arise throughout the day. The point is this: the speech and writing of kindergarten and primary-grade children in connection with any subject of the curriculum are to be recognized as a part of the language program. When the group engages in oral discussion or in cooperative writing, it is desirable for them to be seated in chairs arranged in a semicircle or in even more informal grouping such as clustering on a rug. However, even in an overcrowded, old-fashioned classroom with stationary seats, the spirit of free social communication can readily be developed through careful planning and guidance by the teacher.

INCIDENTAL EXPRESSION

In addition to such periods as are described above, the language arts program includes the spontaneous speech of the girls and boys as they busy themselves with construction and crafts work. In fact, there is no more valuable kind of language than the informal communication of children as they work in small groups on such enterprises as painting, modeling, the making of a movie film, or the preparation of scenery for a dramatization. In such completely informal situations, children make their most effective social adjustment as they develop a feeling of the togetherness of the group that makes them conscious of common interests and that stimulates even the timid child to communicate his ideas, raise questions, and offer suggestions.

Furthermore, such situations provide the opportunity for the teacher to survey the speech habits of individuals and of the group and to determine those language needs that are to be met later by a program of definite instruction. It is to be kept in mind that the major function of the teacher's planned language instruction is *to improve children's natural and spontaneous language.* All children need extended experiences and a richer store of words to express their ever widening background; some may need to improve the voice quality, enunciation, or expressiveness of their intonations; some, to develop a better command of the sentence or perception of the sequence of ideas; certain ones to acquire greater familiarity with the forms of standard English expression; and others to improve in their social adjustment. The instructional program in language must be planned, organized, and administered to meet such needs.

The teacher of the language arts must be as much concerned with *what* children say as with *how* they say it—that is, with *im*pression (intake of ideas) as well as with *ex*pression (outgo). The language arts program must therefore be directed toward two major objectives: (1) the extension and deepening of children's experiences, or provision for the *content* of expression; and (2) guidance and instruction designed to improve the *manner* and *form* of expression.

PROVISION FOR INTAKE

A major responsibility of the teacher in kindergarten and the early primary grades is to increase the range and the depth of children's experiences—that is, to add to the number of items with which they are familiar and t) help them learn more and more about items which they already know too superficially. In so doing, the teacher is helping the children acquire a constantly growing "mental bank account" of ideas that will function both as an *impetus* to expression and as the *content* of speech and writing. A story or poem that vividly portrays an event or an experience may be told or read to the children. By skillful questioning, the teacher can then lead the group to discuss what they have heard, and to relate some personal experiences similar to the one presented in the story or poem. A picture, a filmstrip, or a motion picture will also awaken in the minds of the children various ideas that may serve as meaty content for interesting conversation or storytelling. Trips to local points of interest will provide firsthand experiences in connection with social studies or science. On the other hand, children may be inspired to talk about their everyday experiences outside school: for example, television programs they have enjoyed; books that have been read to them or that they may have read; simple tasks and pleasures in the home; objects they have made; games or play that they enjoy.

Social situations must also be provided in the classroom to offer opportunities for the development of the courtesies, or social language. The expected arrival of a visitor may provide a motivation for developing correct form for greetings and good-bys. A class party may stimulate interest in learning courteous expression in extending greetings, receiving guests, playing games, and the like. In all such experiences, new ideas as to social relationship and responsibility are engendered, and new vocabulary and modes of expression attend upon those ideas.

It is not enough merely to provide children with opportunities to enrich their experience through active, participatory enterprises. They must also become keener and more discriminating in their observation. For example, they should be encouraged to watch quietly while a spider spins its web and snares its first victim, to look at some unfamiliar bird closely so that they can describe it, or to observe how a

An occasional nature walk provides an especially good opportunity for conversation. The teacher should stop periodically to point out things of interest and to encourage questions and comments.

workman uses hammer and nails in order that they themselves may be able to develop better techniques of handling tools safely. It is necessary, then, not only to provide girls and boys with enriching experiences, but also to develop in them the ability to observe more closely various objects, activities, and procedures in their environment.

ORAL AND WRITTEN EXPRESSION

Children need to talk over their observations and experiences in order that their impressions may be strengthened by finding expression in words. The attempt to explain, to describe, or to discuss an experience will, moreover, reveal haziness and gaps in information that point out the need for closer observation to obtain additional information. Therefore, the *intake* of ideas should always be accompanied with a correlative *outgo*, often in words, but sometimes in drawing, modeling, dramatization, or construction.

Most of the expression in kindergarten and the early grades should be oral, partly because the children have not yet mastered the mechanics of written communication (spelling, capitalization, and punctuation), but more largely because occasions for oral expression arise more frequently in real life than do occasions for writing.

The content of oral expression is, of course, of major importance. Yet distinct and accurate articulation and enunciation, simple and clear-cut sentence structure, reduction in crude and illiterate misuse of words, a growing vocabulary, the ability to narrow a topic and to stick to the point—these, too, are objectives to be sought in the children's oral communication.

Until the latter half of the second grade, many children do not have sufficient command of the tools of writing to write for themselves. The teacher must then act as secretary to the individual or to the group and write down the ideas that are expressed. Often a group story or a group report that she has written on the board will be used as a reading chart. In some instances the girls and boys will want copies of their own to carry home, to mail, or to use in a booklet. The youngest may receive duplicate copies, the more mature may copy what the teacher has written for them. It is important to encourage the children to hold to high standards for such copy work—not too difficult a task when their purpose for copying is important to them. Almost surely they will work for neat papers and accurate copying of spelling, punctuation, and capitalization.

Later they will be able to take exercises from dictation and also to complete an unfinished story, both processes serving as steps on the road to independent writing.

Objectives of Language Instruction

In setting up a language arts program that will provide for both impression and expression (intake and outgo), the teacher of young children must plan with definite objectives in mind. These objectives may vary, both as to nature and emphasis, from one locality to another, and some of them may not be fully met until near the end of the second grade. However, certain of them are constant in all situations, and the program of language can be pursued with all of them in mind. These objectives are listed under six categories on the following pages.

Objectives for kindergarten and the first and second grades are very similar in nature, the program in the second grade being directed toward an extension and refinement of those interests and skills that are important in the earlier years. Growth in the power of expression is continuous. As stated earlier in this chapter, some of the abler younger children will be far ahead of the slow-learning and low-average children in second grade. Only in connection with written communication are new skills introduced in the second grade.

I. To enrich the content of oral and written communication
    A. Through firsthand experiences, such as:
        Dyeing fabrics as pioneers did
        Taking trips and excursions for definite purposes
        Collecting specimens
        Setting up and labeling an exhibit
        Entertaining guests
        Having a birthday party
        Caring for pets and flowers, or germinating seeds
    B. Through language experiences, such as:
        Planning the daily activities and evaluating them
        Listening to stories, poems, explanations, and directions
        Using new words acquired through enriching experiences
        Sharing news

     Participating in a show-and-tell period
     Dramatic play and dramatization
     Planning an assembly or party
     Acting as announcer or host

C. Through a stimulating classroom environment that includes:
     A bulletin board for the display of pictures, notices, book lists, children's written stories of special interest
     Pictures featuring current centers of interest
     A book corner with book shelves and a reading table
     A science center in which a museum can be developed
     Supplies to stimulate creative work, including crayons, paints, easels, clay, and simple tools
     Films, filmstrips, and recordings

II. To build desirable attitudes toward listening

A. By fostering group relationships, including:
     Willingness to share ideas and materials
     Sense of responsibility for contributing ideas and effort
     Group rapport that results in ease and confidence
     Cooperative spirit in group enterprises

B. Through provision for successful language experiences, as in:
     Commanding the interest of the group through having something special and uniquely one's own to tell
     Learning new words that help to make ideas clear
     Learning new skills, such as letter form and spelling, as soon as readiness to learn is apparent (but not before)

III. To develop powers basic to expression

A. Through teacher guidance and questioning, directed toward:
     Relating new ideas to old ideas
     Comparison and contrast of observed data
     Assimilation and organization of ideas and facts
     Adherence to the topic under consideration

B. Through development, under the teacher's guidance, of:
     Habits of attentive listening
     A sense of the need for using clear and correct speech
     A sense of sequential organization
     Ability to stick to the point in discussion, group stories, and reports
     A sense of the fitness of the form of expression for various types of written communication, such as labels, announcements, captions for pictures, blank-filling, signs, and lists
     A sense of the need for each preceding type of communication
     A feeling for the importance of using correct forms in writing

C. By encouraging the creative tendencies, in such forms as:
     Original stories, verse, rhythms, dramatic plays, dramatization

IV. To build socially acceptable habits
    A. Through observation of correct practices
    B. Through development in social situations, of:
        The art of give-and-take in conversation and discussion
        Habits of courtesy, attentiveness, and responsibility
        Readiness to accept suggestions and helpful criticism by teacher and classmates
        Use of accepted forms of greetings and thanks

V. To develop desirable speech skills, such as:
        A natural, easy manner and posture before a group
        A clear, expressive, and pleasing voice
        Distinct enunciation and correct pronunciation
        Avoidance of the run-on sentence (overuse of *and, so,* and *then*)
        Elimination of immature speech habits, such as lisping
        Substitution of correct language forms for crudely illiterate ones

VI. To learn and to improve writing skills (largely for second grade)
    A. Through observation of the teacher when writing
    B. Through active participation in writing activities, to develop the following:
        Neat daily written work arranged in correct form
        Neat and accurate copying of announcements and letters (for the slower learners)
        Writing cooperative stories and reports from the teacher's dictation, as a step toward independent writing
        Correct spelling of words frequently used
        Habitual correct use of capital letters and punctuation for such forms of written communication as the group employs
        Habit of checking one's own written work before handing it in

Evaluation by Teacher and by Child

In a complete and wisely conceived language arts program, evaluation is an essential feature. Both the teacher and the children should realize whether or not progress is being made toward the accomplishment of the objectives that have been set up. By studying models and comparing their own language products with such models, by setting up standards, by making tape recordings for evaluative listening, by filing representative samples of work and comparing a recent composition with one written some time ago, and by other means consistent with the nature and purpose of communication, it is possible for the child to make a helpful evaluation of his progress toward the language goals of kindergarten and the first and second grades.

A second-grade group planned to visit the library during the regular story hour in the juvenile room. Before going, they discussed standards of conduct for the trip. Then they listed questions to be used by each child in evaluating his conduct after returning from the trip. Their teacher wrote the questions on a chart, and, after returning from the trip, a period was provided for group and individual evaluation. Here is their evaluation chart:

How Well Did I Do?

On the way
1. Did I walk quietly?
2. Did I keep with the group?
3. Did I talk very quietly?

In the library
1. Did I listen well?
2. Did I thank Miss Wood?

In kindergarten and the first grade and with immature children in the second grade, it is essential for the teacher to assume much of the responsibility for evaluation; to be constructive at all times; to praise creditable achievements of every child, dull or bright, so that a feeling of self-confidence may eventuate; to offer helpful comments that will show each child how and where to improve; and never to find fault, but always to encourage, direct, guide. To the greatest possible extent, abilities of self-appraisal should be developed in the child. Independence in evaluating his own work is a long-range goal for the child in the elementary school.

A teacher will find that making a check list of the accomplishments that are the language goals is a most helpful evaluative device. This check list may be placed on a large chart or on the pages of a loose-leaf notebook. The names of pupils may be placed at the head of columns; the goals may be listed down the left side of the chart or page. Thus the teacher can trace an individual pupil's progress by placing a *plus sign* in the proper square to indicate advancement in a certain area, by putting a *minus sign* to indicate where the pupil needs help, by using a *star* to show unusual proficiency or growth, and by noting a *capital N* to indicate that an explanatory note has been placed in the child's individual record folder to record data and facts that explain the child's problems.

The following chart was devised by one teacher as a means of checking and recording the progress of individual pupils:

PERSONAL DEVELOPMENT

1. Is physically equipped for learning to:
   Listen well (good hearing)
   See well (good eyesight)
   Speak well (normal vocal organs)
   Write reasonably well (motor coordination)
   Participate in general (nutrition, sleep, physical defects)
2. Socially, is learning to:
   Take his turn in group conversation, games, and the like
   Share with others in work or play
   Play and work harmoniously with others
   Assume responsibility
   Work independently
   Follow directions
   Be a leader in at least one type of activity
3. Is emotionally stable, and not:
   Too shy or withdrawn
   Too aggressive
   Subject to temper tantrums
   Subject to fits of depression
   Moody
   Resistant
4. Intellectually, is:
   A slow, average, or quick learner
   Narrow, average, or rich in experiential background
   Particularly interested in __?__
   Lacking in __?__ types of experience
   Observant and curious, or disinterested and phlegmatic
   Resourceful, imaginative and creative; or matter-of-fact

LANGUAGE DEVELOPMENT

1. Listening:
   Has a short, average, or long span of attention

Is developing a longer span
Understands explanation and directions
Follows directions well
Enjoys hearing stories and poems
Gains information through listening
Follows the sequence of ideas
Is a courteous listener when others speak

2. Speaking:
Enunciates well
Has trouble in sounding certain letters
Pronounces words correctly
Has a distinct, pleasing voice
Is easy and poised in manner
Sets off each sentence by itself
Has a varied and growing vocabulary
Uses vivid and interesting words
Arranges ideas in good order
Sticks to the point in group conversation or discussion
Talks in parallel fashion, or can give and take in discussion
Is willing to participate in oral language activities
Is fluent and graphic in oral expression
Is original and creative
Is increasingly correct in use of words
Is replacing illiterate expressions with more acceptable ones

3. Writing:
Is neat in all written work
Is careful in forming letters
Uses punctuation marks correctly
Uses capital letters correctly
Is observant of correct spelling
Is careful to use complete sentences
Is observant of the sequence of ideas
Is interested in learning to write by himself
Is free and spontaneous in writing brief notes and stories

Selected References

EQUIPMENT

Association for Childhood Education International. *Membership Service Bulletin No. 39.* (Lists of materials for nursery, kindergarten, primary,

intermediate; classified lists of tested and approved products, age level, manufacturers; index). 1200 Fifteenth Street, N.W., Washington 5, D.C.
Creative Playthings, Inc. (Dolls, miniature animals, hand puppets). 1 Rockefeller Plaza, New York 21, New York.
Felt for Fun, 2123 Utopia Parkway, Whitestone 57, New York.
Judy Company, The, 310 North Second Street, Minneapolis, Minnesota.

SUGGESTED READINGS

APPLEGATE, MAUREE. *Helping Children Write.* New York: Harper & Row Publishers, 1954.
ASSOCIATION FOR CHILDHOOD EDUCATION INTERNATIONAL. *All Children Have Gifts,* Bulletin No. 100. 1200 Fifteenth Street, N.W., Washington 5, D.C.
———. *Creating Materials for Work and Play Portfolio,* Bulletin No. 2.
———. *Creative Dramatics,* Bulletin 2-A.
ASSOCIATION FOR SUPERVISION AND CURRICULUM DEVELOPMENT. *Creating a Good Environment for Learning,* Chapter 1. National Educational Association, Washington, D.C.
COMMISSION ON THE ENGLISH CURRICULUM. *Language Arts for Today's Children,* Chapter 2. New York: Appleton-Century-Crofts, Inc., 1954.
DAWSON, MILDRED, *et al. Guiding Language Learning.* New York: Harcourt, Brace & World, Inc., 1963.
———. *Let's Talk and Listen.* New York: Harcourt, Brace & World, Inc., 1963.
GREENE, HARRY A. and PETTY, WALTER T. *Developing Language Skills in the Elementary Schools.* 2nd ed. Boston: Allyn and Bacon, Inc., 1963.
LANGDON, GRACE and STOUT, IRVING. *Teaching in the Primary Grades.* New York: The Macmillan Co., 1964.
LOBAN, WALTER D. *The Language of Elementary School Children,* Research Report No. 1. National Council of Teachers of English, 1963.
MCCARTHY, DOROTHEA A., Chairman. *Factors That Influence Language Growth.* National Council of Teachers of English, 1953.
NOELL, DORIS L. "A Comparative Study of the Relationship Between the Quality of the Child's Language Usage and the Quality and Types of Language Used in the Home," *Journal of Educational Research* (November, 1953), pp. 161–67.
REDDIN, MARY E. and GILLESPIE, MARGARET C. *Improving Language Arts in the Elementary School,* Chapters I and II. Columbus, Ohio: Charles Merrill Books, Inc., 1962.
RUSSELL, DAVID and ELIZABETH. *Listening Aids Through the Grades.* New York: Bureau of Publications, Teachers College, Columbia University.

SHANE, HAROLD, *et al.* *Beginning Language Arts Instruction with Children.* Columbus, Ohio: Charles Merrill Books, Inc., 1961.

SHEEHY, EMMA. *The Fives and Sixes Go to School.* New York: Henry Holt and Co., 1954.

STRICKLAND, RUTH G. *Language Arts in the Elementary School,* Chapter 2. Boston: D. C. Heath and Co., 1957.

WILT, MIRIAM E. *Creative Teaching and the Language Arts.* Boston: The Packet (D. C. Heath and Co.).

2
Experience: The Basis for Language Growth

MOST OF the ideas in the minds of young children entering kindergarten or first grade have originated from out-of-school experiences, such as watching Mother and Father at work, helping with certain home tasks, running errands, questioning elders about anything and everything within the range of observation, playing with other children, working in the yard, walking or riding through the country or town, watching television or motion pictures, looking at comic strips and listening as Father or Mother reads them aloud, looking at books and listening to stories read to them from books, shopping with a parent, and taking trips with the family.

The younger the child, the more important are the firsthand aspects of his learning as he acquires informational background through using his hands, his feet, and all his senses of sight, smell, taste, hearing, touch, and kinesthesis (perception of muscular activity). On the basis of many real-life experiences, the child builds a stock of information that enables him to interpret vicarious sources of knowledge, such as picture books or stories he hears. In connection with both his real and his vicarious experiences, there must be discussion and explanation that bring out the meanings in the objects and situations that have come to his attention. Thus concepts grow, the child acquires a vocabulary, and he learns to understand and use sentences competently. Experience, whether actual or secondhand, requires interpretation through language if it is to be accurate and fully understood.

It is important, then, that a young child have a wide variety of

Class trips such as a visit to the zoo are sources for discovery and wonderment that can lead to vivid recollections back in the class.

San Diego Zoo

experiences made understandable through discussion. If his contact with his environment is limited, if little has been done to afford vicarious learnings through books and audio-visual media, or if there has been little talking over of on-going experiences, a child will require much compensatory educational activity in school to fill in the gaps and develop an enriched background. This activity should provide an abundance of language experiences which encourage the child to listen with interest and growing comprehension and to express his ideas freely and clearly. The disadvantaged child may need a long period of experience-building and language development, while his more advantaged classmates forge ahead to more advanced learnings.

A Program of Group Participation

Young children have to live together in school. Heretofore, they have lived in a family whose members vary in age; now they have to share, take turns, follow directions for group activities, and accept personal responsibility. Social demands and opportunities are many; much language learning is involved.

LEARNING THROUGH SHARING

Because the naturally individualistic young child can become a social and cooperative citizen only as he joins with other children in a group enterprise, the teacher in kindergarten and first grade has a particular responsibility for setting up situations that call for group endeavor. The teacher sees that the child helps to keep the play corner orderly, that he works with his classmates in building a class airdrome, or that he helps to plan and carry out a smoothly run trip to the public library.

In all such enterprises, conditions should be such as to contribute to the child's emotional stability. If he is to have a sense of security, he should feel wanted. He should also be so directed that he will have a good chance of being successful. There should be some areas of activity in which he can exercise leadership, but there should be occasions when he recognizes the advisability of following others.

Kindergarten-primary children vary as greatly in their emotional and social backgrounds as they do in their ideational ones. Some are well adjusted socially—that is, they are ready and willing to share with others, to take turns, to be either leaders or followers, to be considerate and courteous, to be responsible and prompt, and to fit in where they may serve the group needs. Others lack one or more of these characteristics because of the lack or the imbalance of earlier training. Some children are too retiring; some, overconfident and even aggressive; some are indifferent to the welfare and happiness of their associates, and generally maladjusted. All vary to some degree in their established interests, though primary children are generally interested in whatever is colorful, concrete, or actively in motion. However, some are more interested in animals and birds, others in policemen and firemen, others in airplanes—the character and type of previous experiences being a determining factor.

DEVELOPING LEARNING HABITS

In the skills and habits that underlie learning, young children also vary. In general, their span of attention is short. The teacher will need to initiate each activity with such appeal as to arouse interest and attention from the beginning, and then to exercise sufficient insight to terminate the activity before interest lags. She should keep periods of learning brief, especially in kindergarten and the early first grade. She can help the children increase their attention span naturally by planning for manipulative activities, by providing for color and movement in the materials she handles, and by appealing directly to the senses.

Children generally need to have their powers of observation sharpened. Whenever an interesting object has been brought to the show-and-tell period, the teacher should steer the children's observation by pointed questions or by comments that direct attention to important features. On a walk around the block or in a park, she may halt the group to notice a swallowtail butterfly flitting among the flowers in a garden, the oriole nest dangling from a twig, or the flash colors of the robin flying across a lawn. In the classroom, she may make up riddles describing one of the children or an object in the classroom. In all sorts of ways, she will help the children to observe closely, to hear, to touch, and then to describe with increasingly keen discrimination.

Listening Activities

Though children learn much through their own observation and active participation, they also learn much through contact with their fellows. They profit from conversation periods in which classmates relate firsthand experiences or reproduce stories and verse heard at home. New interests may be born, social attitudes improved, and concepts broadened as the children tell one another about their personal experiences. Thus it is that listening becomes so important a phase of the language curriculum.

In the sequential development of the four language arts, listening comes first, as the baby hears the sounds about him and gradually learns to attach meaning to them. Thus listening lays the groundwork for subsequently learning to speak, to read, and to write. It is a determiner of a child's speech patterns—the words that make up his preschool vocabulary, his voice quality, his enunciation and pronunciation of words, and his patterns for framing sentences. That is, the child listens to the speech of others and then imitates. This tendency to imitate persists after his entrance into school. Hence the teacher should maintain a desirable quality of voice and speech as a means of improving the oral expression of her pupils and should use prominently the language patterns with which certain pupils should replace their substandard expressions.

Listening is, in fact, as vital and significant a part of the language arts curriculum as are speaking and writing. It provides much of the *intake* so necessary to a rich and effective language arts program. Since there is listening whenever there is talking, occasions in which listening takes place occur throughout the school day. The teacher reads or tells stories and shares poems with the children. Girls and boys volunteer to show and discuss certain pictures in their favorite picture books and to share their individual reading or the stories they have heard at home. There is much to be gained as children converse and discuss experiences in connection with their reading and other learning activities.

RECORDINGS, RADIO, MOTION PICTURES, AND TELEVISION

There are, in addition, some special kinds of listening in the modern primary school. For example, there are recorded poems and stories for children, as well as recordings that give instructions for rhythms and for story plays to accompany music. Outside the school, radio, motion pictures, and television bring enriching opportunities for listening. There are weather reports and even some news items that children can

Slides, films, and filmstrips can often be used to supplement class trips. Children should be encouraged to point out things they have observed, to note details, and to see relationships.

understand. There are literary offerings such as storytelling and dramatizations of stories. Similar opportunities are increasingly provided at the school through the use of radio, record players, and tape recorders in the classroom. The offerings of the community should be noted by the teacher so that she may be alert to such available radio, motion picture, and television programs as will be of value and interest to young children.

TRAINING IN LISTENING

It is highly important that the teacher train children to be thoughtful listeners. If she establishes the practice of giving directions only once—plainly, clearly, impressively—the children soon realize that they are expected to know what to do after a single telling. Some occasions may call for repetition, but in general it should be the teacher's aim to give directions well the first time so that no pupil learns *not to listen* because he expects the directions to be repeated.

Training in listening is especially necessary in these modern times. Most homes have radios and television sets that are turned on much of the time, even when conversation and family discussions are going on. The child must necessarily learn to shut out either the family's talking or the program. He therefore is learning *not* to listen to one thing in order that he may listen to another. Children tend, for this reason, to be quite adept in tuning out what does not interest them, and the teacher needs to be sure that she herself is sufficiently interesting and compelling so that the children do not tune her out, even unintentionally.

WAYS OF IMPROVING LISTENING

The observant teacher knows that she can help children to listen with close and continued attention if she will provide for simultaneous visual appeal so that the eye reinforces the ear; she will associate listening with opportunities for the children to do things, to participate. That is, listening is aided when the teacher takes into account the children's tendencies and their natural interests in active and concrete types of learning.

Children may be helped to grow in listening power if the teacher follows some or all of the following suggestions:

1. Be sure that the children have a purpose for listening, a purpose that is suitable to their level of maturity, to the type of material, and to the occasion. A different mind set is called for as purposes vary. There may be *casual listening* for enjoyment, *intent listening* to ascertain the answer to a question, and *critical listening* to select the best of several stories.
2. Provide a classroom atmosphere conducive to listening: quiet, comfortable, relaxed. Arrange that the young listeners sit as close as possible to the speaker or oral reader.
3. Lead the children to expect meaning in whatever they are listening to. Encourage them to ask questions when they do not understand or when they want further details. Encourage an attitude of mental curiosity.
4. Always prepare the children for listening by recalling related familiar experiences or materials, by developing new words that are likely to be heard, and by questions that arouse curiosity or a feeling of mild suspense.
5. Remember that opportunities to listen for different purposes arise throughout the school day. Take advantage of them.
6. As you talk, write or sketch on the chalkboard. Use clarifying gestures. Listing page numbers, new words, and important points as you present them orally, reinforces listening.
7. Provide for the pupils purposefully to summarize or utilize what they have heard through such follow-up activities as dramatizing, making an illustrative mural or individual pictures, constructing illustrative models, and the like.
8. Help the children to set up a growing list of standards for effective listening so that they will learn when they should listen, how they should listen, and what it is important to remember in specific instances.

Group Experiences Provided by the School

RICH CURRICULAR EXPERIENCES

Naturally the school program should stress firsthand observation and participation in enriching activities. Into the classroom may be brought actual objects, such as a milkweed pod beginning to open and discharge its flyaway seeds, a sprouting bulb, a brooding hen with a nestful of eggs, clusters of frogs' eggs that will produce lively tadpoles, a collection of airplane pictures for a frieze, Indian relics, and many other real things. These may become the objects of directed daily observation and may thus provide timely discussion or conversation and suggest content for group or individual stories or reports.

The children may sometimes be taken out to study the trees on the playground. They may take a trip to a nearby park to observe plant and animal life, or walk around the city block to observe specific neighborhood activities. They may visit a local grocery store in order to make plans for a play store, or visit an airport or a fruit ranch. Numerous possibilities for reaching out into the community to acquire

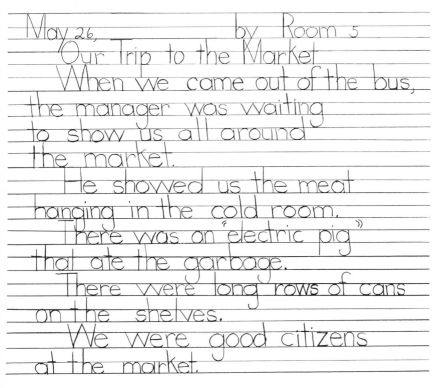

May 26, by Room 5

Our Trip to the Market

When we came out of the bus, the manager was waiting to show us all around the market.

He showed us the meat hanging in the cold room. There was an "electric pig" that ate the garbage. There were long rows of cans on the shelves. We were good citizens at the market.

A class visit to a market produced discussion that resulted in the above story. The children dictated sentences which the teacher wrote on the board. The class chose the best sentences to form the story which they then copied for inclusion in their folders.

new experiences and new ideas present themselves. Perhaps social studies, science, or arithmetic will be the curricular center for certain of these activities. Even so, the language arts program benefits through the enrichment of the children's ideas and vocabulary, improved social attitudes and conduct, the development of keener powers of observation, and growth in the power of selective thinking.

Many of the experiences itemized in the preceding paragraph suggest participation in an integrated curricular program, at least for part of the day. For example, when airplane models have been brought in because of their contribution to a unit on transportation, there will arise the need for an exhibit, entailing classification of objects, arrangement by types, and preparation of legends and labels; invariably, in the progress of the enterprise, there is occasion for discussion of plans and reporting of data. Children learn through observation as well as through doing.

The modern school program affords many other occasions for talking and writing. After pupil helpers are selected to do various classroom chores, plans for accomplishing these chores properly are discussed. Lists of names of committee members are prepared and posted, and there are frequent occasions when the committees' work requires discussion and evaluation. Standards for conduct in the halls, on the stairs, and on the playground are discussed and posted. Each morning the children can participate in making special plans for the day.

Still other activities in the modern school afford occasions for communication. Training in courtesy is essential in any classroom. Children discuss consideration for one another, for example, taking turns, sharing toys and equipment, making the new girl or boy feel welcome, finding a place in the activities for any child who has a tendency to withdraw, and the like. The play period is a particularly fertile source of topics for discussion of such problems as planning for safety measures and for the kinds of play procedures that reflect good sportsmanship.

STIMULATING ENVIRONMENT

Bare walls, desks in straight rows, shelves offering only the required textbooks—these are not the earmarks of a schoolroom where children *live and learn.*

Children usually have many questions when they return from a class trip. Books and illustrations in the library corner encourage them to extend the interest aroused by the trip.

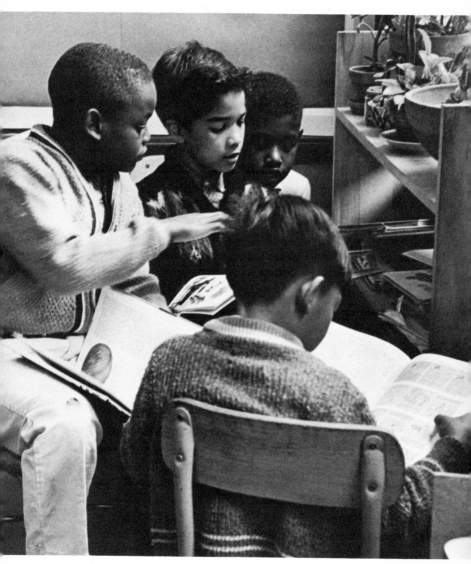

The modern schoolroom has an environment rich in opportunities for learning and in inducements to learn. There are library books on the shelves in a reading corner where the children may browse or seek definite information. There is a display of especially attractive books that the teacher will read to the children. A bulletin board affords an ever changing variety of pictures, announcements, news accounts written by children, or lost-and-found advertisements. From day to day, the children or the teacher will bring in objects of interest to be put on exhibit and to be discussed at appropriate times. Almost always there are living things: a pet or two, an aquarium or terrarium, and flowering plants. Near the school there may be a nature trail with its anthills, frog pond, wild flowers, and bird haunts. Stimulating and rich, but never confusing, is the environment of the school in which children are constantly broadening their background of experience and developing wholesome attitudes and habits of conduct.

VICARIOUS EXPERIENCES

It should be realized that the reading program in itself is a source of language growth. In fact, the reading program is a considerable part of the broader language arts program. As children and teacher share favorite literary selections, the girls and boys gain vicarious experiences. Always there should be discussion preliminary to the reading of a new story; the illustrations should be studied and interpreted. The story is again discussed after the reading. Individual children often volunteer to tell similar stories that they have read, or to relate an experience suggested by incidents in the story. Frequently there is informal dramatization to enhance enjoyment of the story, reinforce comprehension, and heighten appreciation. Thus, reading instruction provides sources of topics for vital expression on the part of children. Simple picture books, filmstrips, recordings, and available textbooks in the social studies, science, or health are equally fertile sources. Truly does the teacher in kindergarten and early primary grades teach language all day long.

An Experience Unit for Grade One

One May day Jerry brought cupcakes topped with single candles to school in honor of his seventh birthday. In announcing the prospective classroom party (which his teacher, Mrs. Murray, and his mother had helped to plan as a surprise for his class), Jerry told how his father, who worked at a bakery, had made these cakes especially for Jerry's birthday party.

The next morning the children dictated the following news story which Mrs. Murray recorded on the chalkboard.

Jerry's Party

Yesterday Jerry was seven years old. He had his birthday party at school. He brought thirty cupcakes for us to eat. Each had a red candle on it. Jerry's father made the cakes at the Taste Good Bakery. They were delicious.

In the discussion that followed the dictation of the news story, the boys and girls asked Jerry many questions about the bakery where his father worked. He answered as well as he could, but the children could not visualize the huge mixing vats and ovens nor understand the processes of preparing baked goods.

Some of the children asked whether they could visit the bakery. On ensuing days there was much discussion about whom to ask for permission to visit, how to ask, when and how to go, what to watch for, and what questions to ask during the visit. Certain children were chosen to discover facts about specific parts of the equipment and the jobs of the different workers. These boys and girls made notes on what they were to ask or observe. After the entire group had helped to plan and dictate a letter of request to the proprietor of the bakery, each child copied it. Then the group chose one letter to send on the basis of neatness, legibility, and correctness.

The subsequent trip with all the preliminary planning for safe and orderly passage to and from the bakery, the visit itself with its demands for careful listening and keen observation, and the ensuing cooperative reports on the pupils' various learnings afforded numerous opportunities for many hours of oral language (listening and speaking) and written records (writing and reading). Many school subject areas were involved: number concepts in terms of time, distances, sizes, and costs; related stories in various books to be read, discussed, and possibly

Imagination and ingenuity in reproducing their experiences often follow a class trip. For example, children may delight in making their own model zoo after visiting a real zoo.

dramatized; songs about bakeries and good things to eat; poems to be spoken in choral arrangements; and art consisting of individual pictures pasted on a long sheet of butcher paper and installed in the pupil-made movie machine. (On this sheet the plainly labeled pictures were arranged sequentially to show the order of activities in the trip.)

Finally, all the first grades were asked to an assembly in which the class presented their learning experiences about the bakery. Planning for the assembly further involved much planning of time, place, means of proffering the invitation, and arrangements for seating. The entire project yielded greatly extended and enriched concepts, additional vocabulary, much social experience, and endless opportunities for using language through listening, speaking, reading, and writing.

Experiences in Grade Two

On the second-grade level, there may be experiences similar to the one outlined for Grade One. One such occasion may be an outgrowth of work in science, such as a walk through the woods, a park, or a garden, or along a hedgerow to observe seeds and seed pods.

Another major experience may concern the study of foods, such as a visit to a neighboring market, with the setting up of a play store or the making of a foods booklet as the outcome. Still others may be connected with the teaching of health and safety, or may concern class events, such as a birthday party or a parents' visiting day.

Countless opportunities do arise, for children's interests are many and varied. The alert teacher will recognize and seize each opportunity. Once an interest is set in motion, the resourceful teacher will see opportunities for (1) enrichment of experience that will awaken the children's minds to new facts and ideas; (2) expansion of meaningful vocabulary; (3) oral expression in the form of conversation or discussion, reporting or explaining, reading stories or poems, and dramatization; (4) different types of recorded expression, such as listed plans, questions, materials, or names; a group or individual news story; picture legends, or labels for exhibited objects; and group stories that recount experiences. In the course of such experiences, the technicalities of oral and written expression for which children in Grade Two have need may be taught with more assurance of permanent learning than can be guaranteed from didactic, separate teaching of isolated skills in which the children have no particular interest. Here are some units that have proved fruitful in many schools:

KINDERGARTEN

Finding My Way	Good Housekeeping
Getting Acquainted	Manners Are Fun
Around the School	Learning to Listen
The Space Around Us	Planning a Garden
Animals for Pets	Holiday Fun

FIRST GRADE

Learning About My Community	Animals of the Fields and Forest
America, My Home	Stories to Play
The People Who Help Us	Taking Care of Myself
Our Bird Friends	Fun and Adventure Stories

SECOND GRADE

Mapping Out Our Community	Where Our Clothing Comes From
Safety on the Big Playground	Exploring Nature
The Bread We Eat	Believe and Make-Believe
A Day at the Dairy	

Selected References

SOURCES OF FILMS AND FILMSTRIPS

Below are the names and addresses of organizations that publish the films and filmstrips listed on pages 44–48. These listings were correct as of the date of publication of this book and the materials listed were available. Commercial organizations do change their addresses on occasion, and, from time to time, publications are discontinued or new ones added.

It is suggested, therefore, that the teacher who is interested in keeping up-to-date on the publication of films and filmstrips secure the latest catalogs from the publishers of such materials.

Before the name of each publisher is an identifying symbol: for example, EBF indicates Encyclopaedia Britannica Films, Inc. These symbols are listed in parentheses after the titles of the suggested films and filmstrips.

ABP   Arthur Barr Productions, 1265 Bresee Avenue, Pasadena 7, California.

AD   Avalon Daggett, 441 North Orange Drive, Los Angeles, California.

AVF   Avis Films, P.O. Box 643, Burbank, California.

BF   Bailey Films, 6509 De Longpre Avenue, Hollywood 28, California.

BFI   Brandon Films, Inc., 200 West 57th Street, New York 22, New York.

BYI   Byron Incorporated, 1226 Wisconsin Avenue, N.W., Washington, D.C.

CASF   Cassard Films, 1511 Penmar Avenue, No. 4, Venice, California.

CC   Charles Cahill and Associates, 5746 Sunset Boulevard, Hollywood 28, California.

CFD   Classroom Film Distributors, 5626 Hollywood Boulevard, Hollywood, California.

CH   Churchill Films, 662 North Robertson Boulevard, Los Angeles, California.

CMC   Center for Mass Communication, Columbia University Press, 1125 Amsterdam Avenue, New York 25, New York.

COPIC   Columbia Pictures Corporation, 1438 North Gower Street, Hollywood, California.

COR   Coronet Instructional Films, 65 East South Water Street, Chicago, Illinois.

CRAIG   Craig Corporation, 3410 South La Cienega Boulevard, Los Angeles, California.

CW   Colonial Williamsburg Film Distributors, Box 548, Williamsburg, Virginia.

DFL   Dennis Film Library, 2506½ West 7th Street, Los Angeles 57, California.

DOW   Pat Dowling Pictures, 1056 South Robertson Boulevard, Los Angeles, California.

EBF   Encyclopaedia Britannica Films, Inc., 1150 Wilmette Avenue, Wilmette, Illinois.

EDH   Educational Horizons, 1730 Eye Street, N.W., Washington, D.C.

FA   Film Associates of California, 11014 Santa Monica Boulevard, Los Angeles, California.

FRITH   Frith Films, 1816 North Highland Avenue, Hollywood 28, California.

GJ   Grover Jennings, P.O. Box 303, Monterey, California.

ICPP   Informative Classroom Picture Publishers, 31 Ottawa Avenue, N.W., Grand Rapids 2, Michigan.

JF   Journal Films, 909 West Diversey Parkway, Chicago 14, Illinois.

JHP	Johnson Hunt Productions, 6509 De Longpre Avenue, Hollywood 28, California.
MCG	McGraw-Hill Films, 330 West 42nd Street, New York 36, New York.
MOODY	Moody Institute of Science, Educational Film Department, 11428 Santa Monica Boulevard, Los Angeles 25, California.
PHP	Paul Hoefler Productions, 1737 North Whitley Avenue, Hollywood, California.
PS	Photo and Sound, 116 West Natoma Street, San Francisco, California.
PYR	Pyramid Film Producers, 1636 North Sierra Bonita Avenue, Hollywood, California.
SD	Sid Davis Productions, 3826 Cochran Avenue, Los Angeles 26, California.
SEF	Sutherland Educational Films, Inc., 201 North Occidental Boulevard, Los Angeles, California.
STEF	Sterling Educational Films, 316 West 57th Street, New York 22, New York.
SVE	Society for Visual Education, Inc., 1945 Diversey Parkway, Chicago 14, Illinois.
TFC	Teaching Films Custodians, 25 West 43rd Street, New York 36, New York.
UMICH	University of Michigan, Freize Building, 720 East Huron Street, Ann Arbor, Michigan.
UWF	United World Films, 1445 Park Avenue, New York 29, New York.
WDP	Walt Disney Productions, 2400 West Alameda Avenue, Burbank, California.
WLF	Wildlife Films, 5149–5151 Strohm Avenue, North Hollywood, California.
WW	Weston Woods, Weston, Connecticut.
YAF	Young America Films, distributed by McGraw-Hill Book Co., Test-Film Division, 330 West 42nd Street, New York 36, New York.

SUGGESTED FILMS

AIR TRAVEL AND THE SPACE AGE

An Adventure with Andy (MCG)

Airplane Trip (EBF)

Airplanes Work for Us (CH)

The Airport in the Jet Age (CH)

The American in Orbit (CRAIG)

Flight of Freedom (BYI)

The Helicopters (EBF)

ANIMALS AT HOME, IN THE CITY, AND IN THE WOODS

Animal Friends (FA)
Animal Hotel (TFC)
Animals of the Farm (CFD)
Beaver Valley (WDP)
Billy and Nanny: The Twin Goats (EBF)
Birds in Your Backyard (ABP)
Care of Pets (EBF)
Farm Animals (EBF)
Farm Babies and Their Mothers (FA)
The Goat Dairy Farm (FRITH)
Horse Farm (GJ)
How Animals Help Us (PS)

Live Teddy Bears (EBF)
Mother Mack's Puppies Find Happy Homes (FRITH)
Our Foster Mother, the Cow (EBF)
Pony Farm (FRITH)
Poultry on the Farm (EBF)
Raccoon's Picnic (EBF)
Sheep and Shepherds (CASF)
Shep the Farm Dog (EBF)
Teddy Bears at Play (DFL)
Three Little Kittens (EBF)
Today's Horse Farm: Sun-Up to Sun-Down (FRITH)

OUR FAMILIES AND FRIENDS

Allen Is My Brother (CH)
Beginning Responsibilities: Taking Care of Things (COR)
Family Teamwork (FRITH)

Good Citizens (EDH)
Home Life (CW) *accelerated groups*
Homes Around the World (UWF)
We Live in a Trailer (BF)

TAKING CARE OF OURSELVES AND OTHERS

Community Hospital (SEF)
A Community Keeps Healthy (FA)
A Community Keeps House (FA)
Eat for Health (EBF) *accelerated groups*
Healthy Families (FA)
Hiking Is Fun (ABP)

Primary Safety: On the School Playground (CRAIG)
Safely to School (CFD)
Stop, Look, and Think (CC)
Strangers (SD)
Why Take Chances? (SD)

LIVING AND WORKING TOGETHER

Apples—From Seedling to Market (EBF)
Behind the Scenes at the Supermarket (FA)
Bread (EBF)
Breadmaking (PHP)
The Bus Driver (EBF)
Cattle Drive (EBF)

City Highways (DOW)
Community Helpers (FA)
A Community Keeps House (FA)
Dairy Farm (FRITH)
A Day with Fireman Bill (FA)
The Doctor (EBF)
Eggs (EBF)
Farmers Make Hay (ABP)

Firehouse Dog (FA)
Helpers in Our Community (CRAIG)
Let's Build a House (CH)
Litterbug (AVF)
The Lumber Yard (BF)
The Mailman (EBF)
Making Bricks for Houses (EBF) *accelerated groups*
Making Shoes (EBF)
Milk (EBF)
The Miller Grinds Wheat (BF)
Pig Tales (FRITH)
Pipes in the House (CW)
Policeman (EBF)

Policeman Walt Learns His Job (FA) *accelerated groups*
Postman Rain or Shine (CC)
Poultry on the Farm (EBF)
The Story of the Wholesale Market (CH)
Streets and the Community (EBF)
Weavers of the West (AD) *accelerated groups*
Wheat Farmer (EBF) *accelerated groups*
Where Does Our Meat Come From? (CRAIG)
Wood (CFD)
Wool (EBF)

MUSIC AND RHYTHM

Basic Movement Education in England (UMICH) (*first 10 minutes show demonstrations of rhythms, etc.*)
Dance Your Own Way (BF)

Railroad Rhythms (FA)
Rhythm Is Everywhere (CFD)
River (PYR)
Toot, Whistle, Plunk, and Boom (WDP)

POETRY

Hailstones and Halibut Bones (STEF)

Whatever the Weather (EDH)

FICTION

Christmas Rhapsody (CFD)
Country Mouse and the City Mouse (CRAIG)
The Golden Fish (COPIC)
Goldilocks (AVF)
Hansel and Gretel (BF)
Legend of Johnny Appleseed (WDP) *accelerated groups*
Little Black Lamb (EBF)

Little Gray Neck (BF)
Niok (WDP)
Princess and the Dragon (STEF)
Pussy Cat That Ran Away (BF)
Rapunsel (BF)
Red Balloon (BFI)
Steadfast Tin Soldier (BF)
Story About Ping (WW)

NATURE AND THE WORLD AROUND US

Autumn on the Farm (EBF)
The Big Sun and Our Earth (CRAIG)

The Desert (ABP)
Finding Out About Rocks (UWF)
The Leaf (PYR)

The Mountains (ABP)
Rocks for Beginners (JHP)
The Seashore (ABP)
Spotty the Fawn (CRAIG)
Spring Brings Changes (CH)

Spring Is a Season (JF)
Treasures in Snow (MOODY)
Wind at Work (DOW)
Winter on the Farm (EBF)

SUGGESTED FILMSTRIPS (FICTION)

ANIMALS WE LOVE

Andy and the Lion (WW–FS9)
Angus and the Ducks (WW–FS39)
The Chanticleer and the Fox (WW–FS26)

Make Way for Ducklings (WW–FS3)
Petunia (WW–FS45)
Three Billy Goats Gruff (WW–FS48)

NATURE STORIES

The Big Snow (WW–FS25)
The Biggest Bear (WW–FS10)
Blueberries for Sal (WW–FS41)
Frog Went a Courtin' (WW–FS28)

Time of Wonder (WW–FS31)
A Tree Is Nice (WW–FS32)
White Snow, Bright Snow (WW–FS24)

LEARNING ABOUT NEW FRIENDS

Crow Boy (WW–FS42)
The Five Chinese Brothers (WW–FS18)
Madeline's Rescue (WW–FS30)

The Miller, His Son and Their Donkey (WW–FS36)
Pancho (WW–FS23)

SUGGESTED FILMSTRIPS (NONFICTION)

WILDLIFE

Mrs. Bear and Her Family (SVE)
Mrs. Cottontail and Her Springtime Family (SVE)
Mr. and Mrs. Mallard and Their Family (SVE)

Mr. and Mrs. Robin and Their Springtime Family (SVE)
Mrs. Squirrel and Her Family (SVE)

SAFETY

Safety on the Bicycle (MCG)
Safety to and from School (CMC)
School Bus Safety (MCG)

Street Safety (MCG)
The Walt Disney Safety Tales (WDP)

ZOO

Trip to the Zoo (YAF)

COMMUNITY HELPERS

Community Helpers Series (YAF)   Our City (ICPP)
   (*set of 6: bus driver, doctor, fire-*   Our Fire Department (EBF)
   man, grocer, mailman, policeman)   Our Police Department (EBF)
Community Helpers (SVE) (*set of 5:*   Our Post Office (EBF)
   baker, fireman, grocer, policeman,
   postman)

BEING AWARE

See and Say (WW–FS52)   What Do You Say, Dear? (WW–
Sparkle and Spin & I Know a Lot of   FS49)
  Things (WW–FS53)

RECORDINGS

Audio Education, Inc., 55 Fifth Avenue, New York 3, New York:
   "How Do You Talk?"   Album ABC10 (*speech skills*)
   Listen and Do Records, Volume III
     "Panda Balloon" and "Jocko, the Dancing Monkey"

Children's Record Guild, 100 Sixth Avenue, New York 13, New York:
   Bring a Song Johnny   CRG 5010   Grandfather's Farm   CRG 5004
   The Carrot Seed   CRG 1003   Train to the Farm   CRG 1011
   First Music for Ones and Twos   Train to the Zoo   CRG 1001

Columbia Records, Inc., 799 Seventh Avenue, New York 36, New York:
   Cinderella   MJ 32   Peter Rabbit   JL 8008
   Jack and the Beanstalk   MJ 31

Decca Records, Inc., 50 West 57th Street, New York 19, New York:
   Manners Can Be Fun 90010

Educational Record Company, Charleston, Illinois:
   Poetry Appreciation Series, Volume I

Radio Corporation of America, Camden, New Jersey:
   The Little Engine That Could   Snow White and the Seven Dwarfs
     (by Paul Wing)   WY 384   WY 33
   Little Nipper, Fire Chief   WY   Winnie and Kanga   Y 439
     2010   Winnie-the-Pooh   Y 438

Simmel-Meservey, Inc., 854 South Robertson Boulevard, Los Angeles 35, California:

Tuneful Tales (by Martha Blair Fox)
- (1) The Laughing Jack-o'-Lantern
  The Nutcracker and King Mouse
  The White Easter Rabbit
- (2) The Shoemaker and the Elves
  The Little Engine That Could
  The Three Little Pigs
  Johnny Cake

Young People's Records, 100 Sixth Avenue, New York 13, New York:

Building a City YPR 711	Muffin in the City YPR 601
Let's Play Zoo YPR 802	Muffin in the Country YPR 603
The Little Cowboy YPR 716	Out-of-Doors YPR 724
The Little Fireman YPR 715	Rainy Day YPR 712
The Little Gray Ponies YPR 735	When I Grow Up YPR 725
Little Indian Drum YPR 619	When the Sun Shines YPR 617
The Men Who Come to Our House YPR 603	Whoa! Little Horses, Lie Down YPR 714

SOURCES FOR FREE BULLETIN BOARD MATERIAL

BOATS

American Steamship Company, San Francisco, California.
Port of New York Authority, 111 Eighth Avenue, New York 11, New York.

DAIRY

California Dairy Industry Education Division, Room 900, 145 South Spring Street, Los Angeles, California.

FIRE HATS

Hartford Fire Insurance Company, 548 South Spring Street, Los Angeles 13, California.

NATURE

Shell Oil Company, 50 West 50th Street, New York 20, New York:
Children Looking for Wonders of Nature.

TRAIN PICTURES

Alcoa Products, Schenectady 5, New York.

BOOKS EVERY TEACHER SHOULD KNOW AND OWN

BREMBECK, COLE. *The Discovery of Teaching.* Englewood Cliffs, New Jersey: Prentice-Hall, Inc., 1962.

HUCK, CHARLOTTE and YOUNG, DORIS. *Children's Literature in the Elementary School.* New York: Holt, Rinehart and Winston, Inc., 1961.

HUMPHREY, ALICE LEE. *Heaven in My Hand.* Richmond, Virginia: Knox Press, 1956.

MERAS, A. *A Language Teacher's Guide.* 2nd ed. New York: Harper & Brothers, 1962.

SHEPPARD, LILA. *Dancing on the Desk Tops.* Evansville, Illinois: Row, Peterson and Co., 1960.

WITTICH, WALTER and SCHULLER, CHARLES. *Audio Visual Materials.* 3rd ed. New York: Harper & Brothers, 1962.

SUGGESTED READINGS

BURNS, PAUL C. "Teaching Listening in Elementary Schools," *Elementary English* (January, 1961), pp. 11–14.

COMMISSION ON THE ENGLISH CURRICULUM. *Language Arts for Today's Children,* Chapter 4. New York: Appleton-Century-Crofts, Inc., 1954.

DAWSON, MILDRED and DINGEE, FRIEDA. *Children Learn the Language Arts,* Chapter 5. Minneapolis: Burgess Publishing Co., 1959.

DAWSON, MILDRED, *et al. Guiding Language Learning,* Chapter 8, pp. 61–69. New York: Harcourt, Brace & World, Inc., 1963.

MACKINTOSH, HELEN, editor. *Children and Oral Language,* pp. 3–21. National Council of Teachers of English, 1964.

RUSSELL, DAVID and ELIZABETH. *Listening Aids Through the Grades,* selected. New York: Bureau of Publications, Teachers College, Columbia University, 1959.

SHANE, HAROLD, *et al. Improving Language Arts Instruction in the Elementary School,* Chapters 3 and 12. Columbus, Ohio: Charles Merrill Books, Inc., 1962.

STRICKLAND, RUTH G. *Language Arts in the Elementary School,* Chapters 3 and 4. Boston: D. C. Heath and Co., 1957.

3
Language Arts
in the Kindergarten

THE TYPICAL kindergarten is a heterogeneous group of children ranging from the culturally disadvantaged to the most privileged, and from the slow-learner to the most able learner. For many children, attendance at kindergarten may be the first major experience of being away from home and mother. For others, it may be a continuation of a nursery school experience or an extension of a planned program in compensatory education. To deal effectively with such diversity is a challenge, indeed, to the teacher and the administrator. But it is a challenge well worth meeting. The curriculum of each kindergarten must be accommodated to the background and needs of all the children in it.

The Kindergarten Child

The more fortunate five-year-old comes to school with an extensive background of information and a host of concepts, with the consequent extensive meaning vocabulary and large speaking vocabulary. Even so, there is need for a further enrichment of experience to fill in and round out his background. The less advantaged child requires a much greater extension and variety of experience that will yield the concepts, vocabulary, and language growth in which he is deficient. Regardless of background, the kindergarten child is likely to confuse fact and fancy and to have made a bare beginning in developing concepts of time

Pictures or other materials that kindle the imagination and invite self-expression help the teacher to guide the language learning of young children. Children in a group like this one can also learn to listen without interrupting, and to respect another child's opinion.

Donna Harris, The Merrill-Palmer Institute

and space. He is an active creature with a curious mind, full of questions, and prone to talk almost endlessly with anyone who is near. He welcomes new experiences and enjoys learning new words that are "handles" for the new concepts he is getting.

Almost any kindergartner watches television and, as a result, has absorbed much information and learned many words that he would otherwise not know. However, much of this intake has probably yielded superficial understandings and faulty knowledge because the viewing has not been followed by questioning, telling, and discussing. The teacher has great opportunity for supplementing, deepening, even correcting what the children see by keeping alert to the programs that they watch, by suggesting worthwhile ones, and by talking over with them what they see and hear.

If a child has traveled extensively, he has much to share with his classmates as he displays his souvenirs and snapshots. If he is fortunate enough to own books of his own, if he lives in a family of readers and has heard many stories at home, he is likely to be much interested in books at school. He will probably enjoy watching the page as a story is read and be able to read the pictures for himself. Almost surely such a child will have an extensive vocabulary and will use language effectively.

Almost without exception, a kindergarten child likes school and enjoys each day's activities. He welcomes general daily routine because he feels secure in knowing what is to come next and in being all set for it. His comparatively short span of attention calls for short and varied activity periods, though a really intriguing experience may last as long as twenty minutes before the child tires or his mind wanders. Increasingly, he learns to finish whatever he starts, but children vary; one will show persistence almost from the beginning of the year while another may need considerable encouragement and guidance over a period of months.

For any kindergartner, the teacher is a parent substitute; the fairly prevalent practice of having both parents work makes this function of the teacher highly important for many a child, who needs the daytime personal interest and attention of an adult. Whether a mother is a housewife all day or not, a child likes to take home the pictures he draws or samples of his crafts; he similarly enjoys bringing from home his toys and books to show his teacher and classmates. Both home and school are important in his life, and he likes to join the two by interchanging possessions in the two locations.

The Objectives of the Kindergarten

The preceding paragraphs have suggested that the kindergarten adds to children's experiences, builds new concepts and extends partially understood ones, and builds language abilities. The kindergarten also contributes to the child's physical and social growth.

In general, the aims of kindergarten education are to promote desirable personality adjustment and to work for all-round development of the child—social, emotional, mental, and physical. The teacher should encourage the children to cooperate in their activities, to share, to take turns, to be leaders and followers by turns, and to be self-reliant, self-directive, and resourceful. As they make a ferryboat from their hollow blocks, play store, feed the rabbit and hamsters, or dust the toys on exhibit, their constant flow of language contributes to social rapport and encourages further language development.

Work with puzzles or with simple tools on a workbench, painting at the easels, modeling with clay, playing on the seesaws and swings, or climbing through the jungle gyms, and playing games such as dodge ball or tag help to increase muscular control and eye-hand coordination. At the same time, such activities help the children to gain social experience, to find emotional outlets, and to be mentally alert.

There are also quiet intake experiences when children listen to stories, observe and listen in the show-and-tell periods, watch films and filmstrips, and enjoy recordings. Talking over reactions to such experiences—if done lightly and briefly—adds to the intake.

However widely kindergarten children may vary in background and ability, they all have the same basic needs. Thus it becomes the aim of every teacher to help all kindergarten children by providing for:

1. Feelings of security and a sense of belonging
2. Multiple opportunities to work with others in planning, sharing, and executing ideas
3. Daily opportunities for academic growth, especially in the

building of new concepts made clear through numerous sensory experiences

4. Numerous occasions for expressing their thoughts and ideas creatively and satisfyingly
5. Situations which fully develop motor skills

The language arts provide better opportunities to meet these needs than any other curricular area.

The Kindergarten Environment

The degree to which the above aims are accomplished depends in part on the environment the school provides. A barren, unhygienic room can actually be damaging; one that is spacious, colorful, cheerful, and stimulating can greatly enhance children's learning and adjustment. The centers for playing house or keeping a store and the stock of large hollow blocks suggest valuable dramatic play. Quiet types of activity evolve from the presence of easels, modeling clay, puzzles, scissors and paste, magnets, rock collections, and other manipulatory materials. On the other hand, lively physical activity results from having swings, jungle gyms, and workbenches.

Many of the preceding activities are individual in nature. Group activities result from the use of a piano, rhythm instruments, recordings and record players, flannel boards, and the chalkboard. The bulletin board with its ever changing displays is a great source of enrichment and a means of extending ideas.

Through a planned environment the teacher sets the stage for exploration. She guides the activities flexibly, leaving room for the children's plans to operate so that new ideas and thinking will flourish.

Setting up the following centers will help to achieve the major objectives of the kindergarten. Naturally, only a few of them will be provided at any one time, and some may last but briefly and be replaced by others which promise to afford experiences and learnings of greater value:

1. Listening center equipped with earphones, jack and plug, tape recorder, and record player

Art experiences develop the aesthetic senses in young children and at the same time stimulate language development. Making accessories for a dramatic play or making a movie box can lead to many understandings related to speech and language.

2. Viewing center that includes a filmstrip projector, slide projector, and a screen
3. Library table with large picture books
4. Art center furnished with easels, brushes, mixed tempera, clay, crayons, newsprint, and newspapers or squares of oilcloth
5. Flannel board plus sandpaper-backed pictures and felt or oilcloth objects for manipulation by children and teacher
6. Puppet corner equipped with stick puppets, finger puppets and/or hand puppets, and possibly a miniature stage
7. Rhythm instrument center with such instruments as coconut shells, sand blocks, tone bells, and shakers
8. Block building center furnished with hollow blocks, floor blocks, orange crates, apple boxes, and large corrugated boxes
9. Housekeeping or store center equipped with child-fashioned box furniture and suitable objects, such as plastic dishes or empty cartons
10. Work center that includes clay and clayboards, cookie cutters, wood, and other supplies and equipment for building
11. Play equipment center that contains beanbags, ropes, a large rubber ball, small balls, and the like
12. Science center which may include a terrarium or aquarium, plants, guppies, turtles, and rock collections
13. Number center with number games, objects for counting, abacus, and puzzles with varied shapes and colors

The centers, when properly used, encourage the development of the following attitudes and purposes:

1. Group cooperation
2. Appreciation of friends and family
3. Courtesy in word and action
4. Respect for the rights and property of others
5. Good health and safety information and behavior
6. Greater awareness of the creatures and objects of the natural world and processes of growth
7. Feelings of security in attempting activities never before tried

If the kindergarten environment and the experiences gained through utilizing the various centers are to yield the desired results, the teacher must have some knowledge of the experiential background of the children. Before she takes them forward, she must take a backward look into their lives. From there she must plan in terms of their needs and interests. It is obvious that needs and interests will vary from child to child; therefore the environment must be varied and rich in its promise and suggestions for activity.

The children need time to adjust to their teacher and new friends. Until now they have lived in a family whose members are of different ages; all at once they are living in a world where all but one or two of their associates are approximately the same age as themselves. They need time to adjust socially as they explore and select from their new environment the equipment and centers which give the greatest personal satisfaction.

Activities in the Kindergarten

At first, each child may wish to react and pursue activities as an individual and gain security as he explores his environment. Later his growing confidence and greater awareness of his associates may lead to group situations where there are joint endeavors in small groups. Activities in the kindergarten should be blocked in relatively short periods, with considerable diversity from one period to another to avoid fatigue or boredom and to provide for the varying needs and interest of the children. Also, since children in one group will differ greatly from their peers in another group because of hereditary and environmental influences, the program from school to school may vary considerably. The daily programs that follow are, therefore, suggestive only.

THE DAILY PROGRAM

In the morning and the afternoon programs that follow, the periods (except for some large-muscle or listening activities) are suitably brief, and quiet and active periods alternate to give variety and to prevent fatigue. It is advisable, of course, to keep a daily program flexible so as to afford opportunities for meeting currently emerging interests and needs. Even so, keeping to approximately the same schedule from day to day is advisable, for, as we said above, children gain a sense of security from knowing what to look forward to as each section of the daily program is carried out.

MORNING PROGRAM

9:00– 9:10	Opening exercises, check on attendance, health inspection, nutrition count
9:10– 9:20	Singing and rhythms
9:20–10:05	Choice of block play, listening center, puppetry, and/or any other centers provided
10:05–10:15	Toilet needs and handwashing
10:15–10:30	Supervised outdoor play—sandbox, jungle gym, gardening, and the like
10:30–11:00	Painting, clay modeling, construction with wood, care of pets, browsing table
11:00–11:10	Clean-up, housekeeping
11:10–11:20	Story time, rhythms
11:20–11:25	Check on day's accomplishments
11:25	Dismissal

AFTERNOON PROGRAM

12:40– 1:10	Outdoor play—sandbox, jungle gym, gardening (on rainy days—large boxes, hollow blocks)
1:10– 1:50	Listening and viewing centers, puppetry, dramatic play
1:50– 2:05	Toilet needs, handwashing, snack
2:05– 2:35	Painting, clay modeling, construction with wood, care of pets, browsing table
2:35– 2:45	Clean-up, housekeeping
2:45– 3:00	Stories, rhymes, check on activities of the day
3:00	Dismissal

BLOCKS OF INVESTIGATIVE ACTIVITIES

The kindergarten teacher should be alert to the spontaneous ideas that children express. Many such ideas may be of sufficient significance to warrant their being incorporated into blocks of investigative activities that may form a background for study in higher grades. For example, a small group's dramatic play and block activities during a free period may reveal interest in airports and planes that has been

Creative rhythms give the entire class a way of expressing themselves. Here, simulating an airplane lets each child explore space in the classroom while carrying out directions.

Ann Zane Shanks

aroused by a weekend visit to watch planes arrive and depart. On such a basis, the story hour, the listening corner, the browsing table, and other centers may feature facts, poetry, and stories about flying.

One teacher used the launching of a rocket as shown on television to interest the children in space, with an immediate aim of developing their space orientation. While playing they were satellites, rockets, and spacemen, they soon discovered they could only twirl around so far before bumping into a wall. This led to their discovery of the four walls surrounding the space making up the kindergarten room.

As large hollow blocks and wooden boxes were brought into use, the children soon learned that they had a limited amount of space into which to arrange them. Thus they were led to experiment in various ways of arranging the blocks and boxes to take best advantage of the available space. For example, they placed the blocks in rows and left wide spaces between each two rows. Eventually they moved the blocks very close together and narrowed the spaces between rows.

As cars, trains, and ships were brought into play, the children found that they needed still more space if they were to park the cars, station the trains, and dock the ships. In addition, any boys and girls who chose to be satellites needed space as they twirled to music. Later the teacher took advantage of these spatial experiences as the children went to the easels to paint. Their concepts of space took on new proportions as they noted that a large sheet of painting paper has four corners. Then, as they worked, they found themselves coloring part of the space and leaving other parts of the paper blank.

These sensory experiences laid a foundation for many later learnings. Large space orientation, the teacher knew, eventually would form the basis for children's noting the smaller spaces between the lines on first-grade writing paper and for understanding the significance of the white spaces between words in a line of print.

The finding and counting of the four walls of the classroom and the arrangement of the building blocks to make long and well-spaced rows would become the basis for understanding arithmetic facts and relationships as well as map studies. As for the children who played satellite and spun around the "earth" or rode their rocket ships to the "moon," they gained an initial understanding of outer space and the men riding through it.

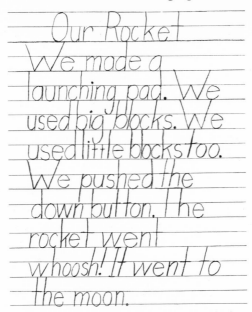

Our Rocket
We made a
launching pad. We
used big blocks. We
used little blocks too.
We pushed the
down button. The
rocket went
whoosh! It went to
the moon.

After building a launching pad with blocks, and acting out dramatic plays, the children dictated this story. The teacher acted as secretary, and each child copied the story.

Ways of Communicating Ideas

Before children exchange ideas, the wise kindergarten teacher will survey their abilities to speak and listen. (Though the teachers in the early primary grades will continue to survey and develop good speech and listening habits, the work should begin in the kindergarten.) There are many informal ways to make the survey. One very effective one is as follows:

A clear plastic box (the kind often used by fishermen) or an empty egg carton is filled with real objects, such as a *b*utton, small *b*all, tiny *c*ar, a *d*ime, a *f*eather, and so on, each in a separate compartment. The children are asked to name these objects in a left-to-right sequence. The teacher notes the following:

1. Movement of the eyes
2. Ability to sound beginning consonants correctly

3. Ability to recognize and name objects correctly
4. Speech and voice habits such as lisping, baby talk, and inability to make sounds correctly

As a continuation training process the children are encouraged to bring objects that are similar in shape, color, and size to the ones shown, as well as objects that are basically the same but differ in shape, color, or size. Such concepts as short, long, bigger, smaller, softer, and smoother may be developed in this way.

Children who may not have objects at home may bring such things as small rocks, leaves, or seashells gathered during leisure time. These contributions may be used in the informal reporting, or show-and-tell periods.

A trip to the pet shop to choose a puppy, a Barby doll given by Grandmother on a weekend visit, a family picnic when a goat raided the lunch basket, the first skiing lesson—such special occurrences may stir a child to informal reporting of out-of-school experiences. In the classroom, he may have fashioned a chair for the play corner from a fruit crate or painted a picture of his new baby brother or fashioned an Easter rabbit from clay. Then he displays and tells about that of which he is so proud.

CONVERSATION AND DISCUSSION

The typical five-year-old is a great talker and may not have learned at home not to interrupt. One of the significant contributions of kindergarten living is his learning to take his turn and to listen with interest to others. As the group plans and evaluates together, the teacher may have to say, "I can't hear when two are talking. It's Sally's turn now," or "We want to hear about Tommy's new hamster, don't we? Let's all listen now." Not only does the child learn not to interrupt, but his preoccupation with "me, my, and mine" lessens, and he moves away from the parallel conversation characteristic of the very young child to the give-and-take of true discussion that underlies group planning and evaluation.

More or less random conversation is replaced by discussion as children have such experiences as viewing filmstrips and films and taking trips. Then the entire class may become involved in orderly discussion.

As the year progresses, the children's attention span and sequential thinking should increase through such discussion.

But the greatest growth in oral language comes out of the conversation among two to four children in their activities in one of the centers. Here they talk freely and listen with interest in real give-and-take conversation as they build with their blocks or arrange a new collection. Often the teacher should unobtrusively place a shy child near an outgoing, friendly classmate who will involve the quiet one in a shared activity and in the consequent conversation.

INFORMAL REPORTING

The widely used show-and-tell period is a time of informal reporting, when a child tells his companions of the observations and experiences of his out-of-school living or displays his painting, crafts, or construction work. No child should feel obligated to participate on a regular basis. Rather, he should speak only when something of real import to him has happened or has been devised. The occasion should be a valuable opportunity for him to share something of worth to his listeners; he should speak spontaneously.

DRAMATIC PLAY

Through dramatic play children acquire many of the characteristics and attitudes that move them toward maturity. It is a truly important means by which they grow into the social environment. Indeed, dramatic play can seem serious business to the five-year-old as he "becomes" Father driving in heavy traffic in the block-built family sedan or the pretended cowboy helping to hold off marauding Indians or a parent scolding the disobedient doll. Or the sounds from the world outside may stimulate his imitation of the barking dogs, the whistling roar of a passing jet plane, the buzzing of an invading bee, or the beep of passing foreign-make cars.

Much of the kindergarten equipment should be of the type to encourage dramatic play: for instance, large building blocks and boxes, furniture of a housekeeping corner, a wardrobe filled with grown-up clothing, and puppets with a simple stage. Puppetry is an especially valuable aid to dramatic play, and children should have many opportunities to use stick puppets made of oaktag or double butcher paper

Dramatic play is a fundamental way to develop imagination and confidence in kindergarten children. A tea party can be very real. A teacher needs ample supplies to encourage children to try out their creative and dramatic ideas.

mounted on lollipop sticks or tongue depressors, hand puppets made from paper bags or stuffed cotton hose, or even finger puppets fashioned from peanut shells. Role-playing of any kind is likely to yield an empathy with the beliefs and feelings of others and will aid the child to grow into his social world in a wholesome way.

Occasionally a group of children may act out a favorite story, sometimes with the puppets, and often with their own bodies. Continuity and sequence of thinking in the use of language are the likely result.

STORYTELLING

Many of the stories that young children tell may be accounts of personal experiences, such as finding a lost dog or having a favorite kite get caught in a tree. Often these stories are told as pupils enter the classroom or paint at adjoining easels. Or personal-experience stories may be shared in the period for informal reporting.

As children learn to go to the book corner and look through the pictures, they should be encouraged to bring a book before their companions and "advertise" it to their friends who would surely like to look at these same pictures. If the book he is displaying is one that has been read to the child at home, he may well tell all or part of its story. Children may also enjoy telling their favorite stories which their fathers or mothers have told them again and again.

Then there will be imaginative children who will make up stories of their own. The bulletin board may often feature pictures that will stimulate such creative thinking. As the school year progresses, there should be more and more of these creative stories, which are enthralling to the young listeners.

An Experience Unit for Kindergarten

Though formal unit teaching is not necessary to a good kindergarten program, a well-developed scope and sequence of an area to be studied is advisable.

I. Initiation of the area to be studied
    A. Children are encouraged to explore the planned environment:
        1. The teacher calls them together after a ten-minute exploration
           period.

2. The children discover many needs:
    To speak to each other
    To play games together
    To count together
B. Many questions arise:
    Where is the lavatory?
    Where can we get a drink?
    When do we have milk or orange juice?
    Where do we play?
    Who brought all these playthings and supplies?
    When can we use them?

II. Planning to solve problems together
    A. The teacher and children plan a trip around the school yard to answer questions.
    B. Many other questions arise:
        How many may play on the jungle gym?
        How many may play in the sandbox?
        How far on the playground may we go?
        What are the large apple boxes and orange crates for?
        Why can't we go into the big yard?
        How can we find our way back to our room?

III. Beginning to solve problems together
    A. Number concepts may be formed and developed slowly:
        The number of people in our class
        The number of our room
        The number on the lavatory door
        The time we come to school
        The time we go home
        The money we need for our milk or orange juice
        The number of children in the sandbox
        The number of children on the jungle gym
        The number of our coat hanger
        The number of quarts of water for the terrarium
    B. Quantitative concepts are introduced:
        The size of the floor blocks
        The quantity of blocks and books
        The size of the playground and play area
    C. Space relations are acquired together:
        The room has four corners.
        There are left and right directions.
        There is up and there is down.
        There are in and out.
        There is space around us.

D. Listening to directions and following them is stressed:

> Follow the directions in the games in the classroom and the play yard.
> Listen to the rhymes, stories, and songs.
> Tap out rhythm according to directions.
> Twirl, glide, fly, or spin according to the way the music makes one feel.
> Plan how to express ideas. Then show others how to do the same.

IV. Working and looking together
   A. The teacher shows still pictures, slides, or filmstrip of unit being worked on.
   B. The children work on spaceship and launching pad:
   > Painting a big box as a blockhouse
   > Building the launching pad with blocks
   > Making satellites of clay
   > Painting pictures of spacemen, planets, etc.
   C. The children evaluate their activities and plan for the next day.

V. Learning and playing
   A. The children dramatize the launching:
   > The countdown—10, 9, 8 . . .
   > (*Children may cover eyes and try to guess who is giving the countdown, and may walk single file behind the leader to the launching pad.*)
   > Fueling for the takeoff
   > Picking up the spaceman from the landing place
   B. They evaluate and modify the dramatization.

VI. Housekeeping
   A. The children clean the area in which they have worked.
   B. The children put all the equipment in place.

VII. Returning to chairs or places on the floor
   A. The children say good-bye to everyone.
   B. They later help to clean up.

Selected References

SOURCES OF FILMSTRIPS

CMC   Curriculum Materials Corporation, 1319 Vine Street, Philadelphia, Pennsylvania.

EBF   Encyclopaedia Britannica Films, Inc., 1150 Wilmette Avenue, Wilmette, Illinois.

JH   Jim Handy Organization, 2821 East Grand Boulevard, Detroit 11, Michigan.

MCG   McGraw-Hill Films, 330 West 42nd Street, New York 36, New York.

SVE   Society for Visual Education, 1345 West Diversey Parkway, Chicago 14, Illinois.

WDP   Walt Disney Productions, 2400 West Alameda Avenue, Burbank, California.

YAF   Young America Films, Inc. (McGraw-Hill Films), 330 West 42nd Street, New York 36, New York.

SUGGESTED FILMSTRIPS

WILDLIFE

Mrs. Bear and Her Family (SVE) Mother and Father Bear with their children in seasonal activities, building a dam, making their winter home.

Mrs. Cottontail and Her Springtime Family (SVE) Mother Rabbit builds her home and her babies grow to maturity.

Mr. and Mrs. Mallard and Their Family (SVE) The Duck Family from the time they try their wings until they are fully grown.

Mr. and Mrs. Robin and Their Springtime Family (SVE) How the robins plan their homes by instinct; describes growth pattern of baby robin.

Mrs. Squirrel and Her Family (SVE) How squirrels find and store their food and how they protect themselves from danger.

SAFETY

Safety on the Bicycle (MCG)
School Bus Safety (MCG)
Street Safety (MCG)
Safety to and from School (CMC)
The Walt Disney Safety Tales (WDP) (*an introduction to school safety*)

ZOO

Trip to the Zoo (YAF) (*an interesting and complete study of the zoo*)

RECORDINGS

STORIES TO HEAR

Crest Records, Inc., 220 Broadway, Huntington Station, New York:
   The Fox and the Grapes   Crest CT–2

The Frog and the Ox
The Tortoise and the Hare

Mercury Record Corp., 35 East Walker Street, Chicago, Illinois:
The Elves and the Shoemaker   Mercury MMP–16
The Fisherman and the Flounder

Capitol Records, 1750 North Vine Street, Hollywood, California:
Puss in Boots and other Stories
for Children   Vol I (Capitol CD–11)

PARTICIPATION RECORDS

Educational Record Sales, 157 Chambers Street, New York 7, New York:
Eensie Beensie Spider
Mouse and the Frog
Songs of Safety

Young People's Records, 100 Sixth Avenue, New York 13, New York:
The Big Engine   Parade
Looby Loo   Wintertime

Children's Record Guild, 100 Sixth Avenue, New York 13, New York:
Sunday in the Park
   Walking Song
   Stretching Song
   Rolling Song

Record Guild of America, 16 West 40th Street, New York 18, New York:
My Playful Scarf

Little Golden Records, 630 Fifth Avenue, New York 20, New York:
Syncopated Clock

Pacific Records, c/o Children's Music Center, Inc., 5373 West Pico Boulevard, Los Angeles, California:
Listen and Learn   Album AC 120

Bowmar Records, 10515 Burbank Boulevard, North Hollywood, California:
Singing Sounds—Books 1 and 2
(Give an interesting approach to the presentation of the alphabet. A
series of records with a book of verse to follow along with kindergarten
Exchange of Ideas.)

Simmel-Meservey, Inc., 854 South Robertson Boulevard, Los Angeles 35,
California:
Nutcracker Suite

FOR RHYTHM INSTRUMENTS

Ginn & Co., Statler Building, Park Square, Boston 17, Massachusetts:
Sleep, Baby, Sleep (tone bells—number notation) Ginn-First Grade
Jimmy Crack Corn
Listen and Sing
Together We Sing

LISTENING CORNER EQUIPMENT

Headphones; Educational Headset. Available at local electronic or audio-visual dealers, or from the following dealers:

> Radio Product Sales
> 1501 South Hill Street
> Los Angeles, California
>
> Radio Specialties
> 1956 South Figuerva Street
> Los Angeles, California

SUGGESTED READINGS

AVERY, MARIE and HIGGINS, ALICE. *Learn How to Learn.* Los Angeles: Times-Mirror Syndicate, 1961.

BANHAM, KATHERINE M. *Maturity Level for School Entrance and Reading Readiness.* St. Louis: Educational Publishers, Inc., 1959.

BLAKELY, PAUL and SHADLE, ERMA. "A Study of Two Readiness-for-Reading Programs in Kindergarten," *Elementary English,* November, 1961.

FOSTER, JOSEPHINE and HEADLEY, NEITH. *Education in Kindergarten.* Revised edition. New York: American Book Co., 1959.

HEFFERNAN, HELEN and TODD, VIVIAN. *The Kindergarten Teacher.* Boston: D. C. Heath and Co., 1960.

————. *The Years Before School.* New York: The Macmillan Co., 1964.

HILDRETH, GERTRUDE. *Readiness for School Beginners.* New York: Harcourt, Brace & World, Inc., 1950.

HYMES, JAMES L. *Before the Child Reads.* Evanston, Illinois: Row, Peterson and Co., 1958.

LANGDON, GRACE and STOUT, IRVING. *Teaching in the Primary Grades,* Chapters VI and VII. New York: The Macmillan Co., 1964.

LAMBERT, HAZEL M. *Teaching the Kindergarten Child.* New York: Harcourt, Brace & World, Inc., 1958.

MARGOLIN, EDYTHE. *Who Leads the Kindergarten Sub-Culture?* University of California at Los Angeles, 1965.

MC KEE, PAUL, *et al.* *Getting Ready to Read.* Boston: Houghton Mifflin Co., 1962.

MERRITT, HELEN. *Guiding Free Expression in Children's Art.* New York: Holt, Rinehart and Winston, Inc., 1964.

RUDOLPH, MARGUERITA and COHEN, D. H. *Kindergarten: A Year of Learning.* New York: Appleton-Century-Crofts, Inc., 1964.

UNITED STATES OFFICE OF EDUCATION. *Educating Children in Nursery Schools and Kindergarten,* Bulletin No. 11, 1964.

WITTY, PAUL and SIZEMORE, ROBERT. "Studies in Listening, a Postscript," *Elementary English,* May, 1959.

4

Informal Oral Communication in the Early Primary Grades

MUCH OF the oral communication of children in the early primary grades is completely spontaneous and unplanned. In the play corner, at the easel, and during constructional activities, the children quietly chat and talk over their plans. Often, with little or no planning, they will play the story they have just read or heard. The educational values of informal oral communication are high because through such spontaneous interchange of ideas children grow socially and emotionally.

Ways of Communicating Ideas

EXCHANGING PERSONAL NEWS

In the early primary grades, it is common practice to begin the school day with a short exchange of news items among the pupils. Often a bit of news is so important or appealing that it is selected for "News of the Day," a story dictated to the teacher and put on the chalkboard for subsequent supplementary reading. This selection comes as the result of the discussion stimulated by the various news items and the evidence of the pupils' interest in a particular one. The spontaneous reporting,

Finding countries or oceans or mountains on a globe can provide much pleasure for young children and leads to informal oral exchanges of ideas.

the accompanying discussion, the planning of the sequence for recording the story, and the final dictation make up valuable features of the daily oral-language activities. (Advanced pupils at the second-grade level may prefer to write out a personal item which they have related and the class has chosen as the one important and interesting enough to be featured that day. Oral-language activities are involved as each writer is given an opportunity to read aloud what he has written, and the class makes suggestions for supplementation or revision. Such oral reading and the resulting discussion are important types of oral communication.)

Many schools provide for a show-and-tell period at any time that a pupil voluntarily brings something he very much wants to show and explain, for example, a birdhouse he has made or some gift he has just received. Really purposeful show-and-tell experiences are valuable avenues for extending and enriching children's concepts and vocabulary as well as for setting up lifelike situations for actual communication of ideas through speaking and listening.

Informal Atmosphere   The atmosphere for the news or the show-and-tell period should be as informal as possible, with girls and boys seated in their chairs in a semicircular group, or perhaps seated on a rug, with the teacher sitting on a low chair nearby. Individual children present their items, preferably not raising their hands for recognition before speaking. The teacher should be unobtrusively in control, inviting each child who is ready with news or an exhibit to take his turn. Yet always she should guide with the following objectives in mind:

To inspire voluntary expression by question and suggestion
To see that no child does more than his share of talking
To encourage a backward child to talk
To instill good listening habits
To lead children to question one another

As far as possible, she should let the children proceed without being conscious of outside direction. For the overtalkative child, however, there may be a quiet reminder that Jackie has something to display

and should have a turn soon and, for the timid one, kindly and stimulating questions that will break the reserve.

Usually a child's presentation of news will be quite brief, but there
may be an occasion when he has reason to speak at considerable length.
He may have fed the animals at the zoo or have become separated
from his mother in a large department store. The nature of a show-
and-tell period will vary with the character of the items the children
have to report; it will probably come irregularly since it is appropriate
only when an individual child has had an experience sufficiently unusual and interesting to make his sharing valuable to his classmates.

CORRECTIVE WORK

At the kindergarten-primary level, the teacher will be alert to note
the speech needs of the children, and will try to meet these needs posi-
tively. If vocabulary is meager, she will introduce requisite words as
real and vicarious experiences provide the knowledge and understanding desired. If a word is poorly enunciated, or if a gross and illiterate
type of error is made, she will attempt to make the correct forms con-
spicuous in her own speech and oral reading and to incorporate the
correct forms in reading charts. Thus through their listening and oral
reading, the children will tend to become more and more accustomed
to the correct forms and eventually to use these imitatively in their own
speech. Improved sentence structure may be learned in the same way;
also the teacher may phrase her questions so that sentence answers are
encouraged. For instance, she will use *how* and *why* questions, rather
than the *who, when,* and *where* types. Simple choral speaking of
rhymes and short poems may give incidental help in enunciation, pronunciation, and voice intonations in such a way that no child feels
self-conscious as he endeavors to say his words and sentences exactly
as the other children do, as many voices blend in a harmonious, clear-
cut fashion.

Occasionally, in late first grade or in the second grade, the teacher
may feel justified in making corrections at the time an error is made
or very soon thereafter. For instance, if a certain gross and illiterate
type of error has received considerable attention in previous weeks,
she might, during the news period, give immediate correction by saying, "You *saw* a jet plane, Jimmy. Say *saw*, not *seen*." This should be

done quietly, in a manner that will not embarrass Jimmy or repress his desire to speak. Preferably, she will go quietly to Jimmy's side and say, "You forgot to say *I saw* this morning, Jimmy. Please tell me again what you *saw* last Sunday." This is so handled that the other pupils are unlikely to notice.

DRAMATIC PLAY

In dramatic play, a child impersonates someone else and so thoroughly identifies himself with the character that in his imagination he becomes that person. He thinks and behaves as if he were actually someone else.

Dramatic play ordinarily involves no story or plot. Children are engaging in dramatic play when they play school or store; when they dramatize Indians by sticking feathers in their hair; when they dress up in their parents' clothing and imitate their elders; when they pretend they are keeping house, running a store, or driving a fire truck, a bus or streetcar, or a racing automobile; and when they set up a play post office and deliver mail. Young children spend much of their playtime at home in dramatic play. At school, there should be large blocks for building an airport or a garage, dolls for playing house, some materials for costuming, toy trucks and drums, and other play materials that stimulate the children's imagination and encourage them to dramatize interesting activities in home or community. Such dramatic play may be pursued at recess time, if need be; better still, it may take place during free periods in the day's program.

The children in one first grade came in from their morning play period and scattered to various interest centers around the large room. Four little girls went at once to a large wooden box from which they extracted some articles of clothing for an adult. They were soon garbed in long dresses and high-heeled shoes and carried big purses. One child was seated in the play-corner living room, ready to receive callers. When a knock came, she received her guests in a truly adult manner. Then there followed the kind of chitchat that they heard when their mothers had callers at home. Soon there was a serving of make-believe tea and cookies. Any mother, as well as any teacher in a modern first-grade classroom where children have some free playtime, can cite many

Dramatic play helps children to adjust to various social situations and gives the teacher new insights into the interests and the language patterns of each child.

similar incidents of boys and girls engaging voluntarily in dramatic play that momentarily seems very real to them.

Dramatic play has many values. To the child, it is a means of gaining an understanding of the adults he meets in his daily activities. Through his identification with them, he is taking strides toward becoming an intelligent and active member of a family and citizen in a community. Through dramatic play, the child learns about the common problems of group living, about fair play, and about the give-and-take of family living. Such play also aids the child in adjusting to the social situations that life brings. Perhaps fully as important are the release of tensions and the expression of repressed feelings.

To the teacher of the child, there are equivalent values. She may glimpse the tensions and problems that explain deviations in the behavior of individual children. Also revealed are the interests, special abilities, aptitudes, or needs of a child. The teacher can see what language patterns the child is developing and what he lacks in vocabulary and sentence mastery. She can help the boy or girl grow into a more stable, well-rounded personality if she is thus sensitive to the revelations of children's dramatic play.

DRAMATIZATION

A truly valuable type of oral communication is the spontaneous dramatization of a story which the children have just read or have heard the teacher read or tell. A teacher interested in developing, within her group, such qualities as spontaneity, fluency, imagination, originality, and constructive social attitudes will frequently let them play their stories with little or no previous planning and with a minimum of direction.

Preferably, the suggestion that the story be played should come from the group. If the action and conversation are simple enough, the children can proceed to choose a cast that will play the story. In more complex situations, there may be discussion of the setting of the story, of the principal train of events, and of the dialogue. Such informal dramatization is fun, and the spirit of spontaneity and enjoyment should not be dampened by criticism.

When time is available, more than one cast of characters may work out a dramatization. The second group may go to the hall, the cloakroom, or a far corner of the classroom to plan their own version of the play. Thus, each cast is enabled to present its own conception of the story without being unduly influenced by the other cast of characters. Children who do not appear as actors will enjoy being the listening audience. They may at times help to appraise each presentation and to select a final cast, provided that the children wish to present their play to another class or to visitors in the classroom.

A typical dramatization   After reading "The Elves and the Shoe-maker," one second-grade class suggested that they play the story. Because the children had already discussed the story in spirited fashion and had enjoyed their dramatic reading of selected parts (choosing a lively part to read aloud and then calling on one or more classmates to pantomime this part), the teacher felt that any detailed planning of the dramatization was unnecessary. Some children did suggest that the shoemaker squat atop a table, that he put one of a pair of galoshes on the top of a handy gallon tin can, and that he use the handle of a large pair of scissors for a hammer. They also suggested that a nearby screen be used as the door about which the characters would peep to watch the making of shoes by either the shoemaker or the elves. Several children then volunteered to take the parts of the respective characters and act out the play.

Afterward, the entire group evaluated the play, first expressing praise for the completeness and good sequence of the action and conversation used by the impromptu players. However, it was felt that the elves hadn't sounded as elves would, and several children gave their versions of the voices of elves. Then a second cast was chosen, and the suggestions were carried out, using the preferred way of speaking in elf-fashion. The little play was so popular that groups of second graders formed at recess time and acted out the dramatization in a lively manner. Eventually a cast was chosen to present the play at a pre-Christmas party for parents.

Story and Poetry Hour

There should never be a day when the teacher fails to read or tell a story, to read aloud from a book that is being presented a chapter at a time, or to read and recite choice bits of verse to or with her pupils.

The story hour should be a highlight in the school day. The selection of story and verse should be varied so that the children may sometimes be highly amused, sometimes filled with enthusiastic approval, often curious, usually held by real suspense, and occasionally indignant. Imagination, or the ability to build mental pictures, should be stimulated by the literature that the teacher presents. Standards of conduct and ideals of human relationships may be instilled during such periods and horizons of thought and insight gradually extended beyond the local community to peoples in faraway times and in distant places. One of the greatest benefits, however, is the likelihood that a love for reading will be encouraged and that the school will not only teach children to read, but to *be readers* in the years to come.

PREPARATION BY THE TEACHER

Whether the teacher is to read or to tell a story, she must prepare thoroughly. She is the go-between for the author and her listeners and has the responsibility for conveying plot, action, characterizations, and moods with the meaning and spirit the author intended. This means that she must be fluent, expressive, and stirring in her presentation. By becoming thoroughly familiar with a story, she can frequently lift her eyes from the printed page as she reads and thus gain eye contact with the children. Her face can express her inner response to the emotional situations portrayed in the story; then their attention is likely to be close and sustained.

Much as boys and girls delight in hearing a story read, they derive even more enjoyment from hearing it told. In fact, authorities in story-telling maintain that most stories should be told rather than read aloud. The teacher should read directly from a book only if, by telling it, she cannot do justice to a story's unusual vocabulary (as with many of Dr. Seuss's books) or artistic style (like that in *The Little House* by Virginia Lee Burton). An effective kindergarten-primary teacher almost surely has a rich repertoire of stories to tell. These she uses not only in the story hour but also in occasional moments when, for one reason or another, a brief period of free time occurs.

Even more crucial is the teacher's preparation for reading poetry because, if she is not careful, the rhythm of the lines and the melody of the words may induce her to read in singsong fashion so that meanings

The teacher should read aloud or tell a story every day. Children's interests and reactions vary greatly so stories and verse should also vary, sometimes being light and amusing, sometimes suspenseful, sometimes serious or even sad.

are concealed rather than revealed. Before presenting verse, she must think through the theme of the poem, consider the sense of the lines, respond to the mood, probably rehearse, and then read to the children in such manner as to highlight meaning and feeling as expressed by the poet. For instance, Robert Louis Stevenson's "Where Go the Boats?" should not be read as a succession of rhythmic, tuneful phrases so that the listeners are left with a vague impression of pretty music in metrically arranged words. Rather, the teacher should bring out meanings through intonation as she raises the pitch of her voice slightly on the key words and possibly pauses very slightly after such words in order to make them even more impressive. There is no loss in musical effects when meaning is thus highlighted. In fact, the children can sense vividly the sight and sound of an imaginary river flowing, flowing, and, in its course, carrying a child's boats far away to other children playing on its beaches.

The meaningful intonations and pauses of "Where Go the Boats?" are shown below. The words in capital letters are the ones to be spoken in a somewhat higher pitch; a caret indicates the place where the tone should be sustained and a slight pause may add to the impressiveness of an idea. Try reading the poem with intonations and pauses as indicated. Remember that a comma or dash calls for a more noticeable pause than a caret, and a period or a question mark indicates a distinct halt. Never hurry the reading of a poem because listeners require time to absorb the meanings in the "poetic" wording.

> Dark BROWN ∧ is the RIVer,
>   GOLDen ∧ is the SAND.
> It flows along FOREVER,
>   With TREES on either hand.
>
> GREEN LEAVES ∧ a-FLOATing,
>   CASTLES of the foam,
> BOATS of mine a-BOATing—
>   WHERE ∧ will all come HOME?
>
> On ∧ goes the RIVer   (*no pause*)
>   And OUT ∧ past the MILL,
> AWAY ∧ down the VALLey,
>   AWAY ∧ down the HILL.

AWAY ∧ down the RIVer,
  A HUNDRED MILES ∧ or MORE,
OTHER little children   (*no pause*)
  Shall BRING ∧ my boats aSHORE.

SELECTION OF POEMS

The kindergarten-primary teacher should always have a large variety
of poems on hand. If the children have seen a squirrel scampering up
a tree or sitting on a limb cracking a nut, she might read "The Squirrel,"
which tells how the lively creature goes "whisky, frisky" up the tree and
opens the nut shell "snappity, crackity." Or, if she has noticed the
pupils shuffling through the leaves on the way to school, "Autumn
Woods" by James Tippett is timely. Always her choice should be made
according to the maturity of her group. The thought should be simple
and childlike and the rhythm marked, though rhyming lines are not a
necessity. Children revel in rhythm and lilt, and they often enjoy a
poem that has unfamiliar words, provided the ideas and the imagery
are sufficiently simple and appealing. Harry Behn's "Hallowe'en" is a
case in point because Hallowe'en is a favorite holiday, and the children
can respond to the spirit of the night—

> When elf and sprite
> Flit through the night
> On a moony sheen. . . .
>
> When leaves make a sound
> Like a gnome in his home
> Under the ground,
> When spooks and trolls
> Creep out of holes. . . .*

The short lines, the frequent rhymes (both internal and end-of-line),
and the staccato perfectly reflect the suspense and fun of the holiday.
Children delight in words that portray sounds, such as the bell
sounds in "Ding, Dong, Bell," or the sound of the ticking of the clock
in "Hickory, Dickory, Dock." They delight in marked rhythms, such as
the beat of horses' hoofs in—

---

* HALLOWE'EN: From *The Little Hill* by Harry Behn. Reprinted by permission of
Harcourt, Brace & World, Inc., New York.

> Ride a cock-horse to Banbury Cross,
> To see an old lady upon a white horse.

or the rocking rhythm in—

> Bye, baby bunting,
> Daddy's gone a-hunting.

They are also intrigued with marked rhyming. In searching for poetry for young children, therefore, the teacher must bear in mind the children's love of "sound" words and of marked rhythm and rhyming. Most of the Mother Goose rhymes embody these characteristics, and, consequently, they provide good introductory material for Grades One and Two. The list that follows includes a number of Mother Goose rhymes and also some other rhymes or verse for children. Most of them may be found in the anthologies and books of verse listed at the end of this chapter.

DRAMATIZATION

"Annie the Elephant," by Carrie Rasmussen

"Christmas Presents," by J. J. Thompson

"Ride a Cock-Horse" (Mother Goose)

"Little Miss Muffet" (Mother Goose)

"Passenger Train," by Edith Newlin

"The Kitchen Clock," by Barbara Young

"Wee Willie Winkie" (Mother Goose)

"I Had a Little Pony"

"Pease Porridge Hot" (Mother Goose)

"Shore," by Mary B. Miller

"Singing-Time," by Rose Fyleman

"Marching Song," by Robert Louis Stevenson

"Row, Row, Row Your Boat" (author unknown)

"My Balloon," by J. J. Thompson

"The Christmas Pudding" (Mother Goose)

ALLITERATION

"Alphabet Sounds," by Marilyn Hickson, Pauline Foster, and Dorothea Hodgkinson

"Georgie, Porgie, Pudding and Pie" (Mother Goose)

"Goosey Goosey Gander" (Mother Goose)

"Holes in My Shoes," by Barrows and Hall

"Wee Willie Winkie" (Mother Goose)

"The Scissor-Man," by Madeleine Nightingale

"Sing a Song of Six Pence" (Mother Goose)

"Godfrey Gordon Gustavus Gore," by William Brighty Rands

"Higgledy Piggledy, My Black Hen"

(Mother Goose)

"C is for the Circus," by Phyllis McGinley

"P's the Proud Policeman," by Phyllis McGinley

RHYME

"Hickory Dickory Dock" (Mother Goose)

"Holding Hands," by Lenora M. Link

"What Does Little Birdie Say?" by Alfred, Lord Tennyson

"Old King Cole" (Mother Goose)

"Little Polly Flinders"

"Zebedee, the Zebra," by Christie Jeffries

"This Happy Day," by Harry Behn

"Time to Rise," by Robert Louis Stevenson

"The Three Foxes," by A. A. Milne

RHYTHM

"The Swing," by Robert Louis Stevenson

"One, Two, Buckle My Shoe" (Mother Goose)

"Summer Rain," by Louise Abney

"As I Was Going Along" (Mother Goose)

"B's the Bus," by Phyllis McGinley

"Hurdy Gurdy," by Eleanor Farjeon

"Master I Have" (Mother Goose)

"Little Wind," by Kate Greenaway

IMAGINATION

"The White Window," by James Stephens

"Bundles," by John Farrar

"My Book Holds Many Stories," by Annette Wynne

"Randy Rocket," by Judith N. Flynn

"The Cat's Tea-Party," by Frederick E. Weatherly

"The Candy Store," by Marian Kennedy

SENSORY APPEAL

"Sounds at the Ball Game," by Judith N. Flynn

"Smells," by Christopher Morley

"The City Things," by Lucy Sprague Mitchell

"The Fireman," by Grace Baker

"The Wind," by Robert Louis Stevenson

"Stop-Go," by Dorothy Baruch

"Traffic Sounds," by James Tippett

"Roads," by Rachel Field

"Trains," by James Tippett

"Carrying the Mail," by Lola Dunnavant

"Airplane Landing," by Dorothy Baruch

"Where Go the Boats?" by Robert Louis Stevenson

"It Is Raining," by Lucy Sprague Mitchell

"Ice," by Dorothy Aldis

"Airplanes," by Mary Louise Allen

"Boats," by Christina Rosetti

"The Baby Goes to Boston," by Laura E. Richards

"My Valentine," by Mary C. Parson

"The Big Clock" (author unknown)

"Bakeshop Window," by Marian Kennedy

MOTION

"Space Pilot," by Alice Landon

"Merry-Go-Round," by Dorothy Baruch

"Jump, Jump, Jump," by Kate Greenaway

"The Little Turtle," by Vachel Lindsay

"Taking Off," by Mary McB. Green

"Hayride," by Muriel Schulz

"The Dolly Walks and Walks," by S. N. Coleman

The teacher should read poems in such a manner as to portray the enjoyable features of each. Several poems related to a current interest may be read at one period. For example, when a unit related to farm life is in progress, Stevenson's "The Cow" and Elizabeth Madox Roberts' "The Hens" may be read. After the children have engaged in dramatic play during a free period, the teacher may read Stevenson's "A Good Play" and Dorothy Aldis' "Hiding."

SOURCE OF MATERIALS

No teacher's professional library is complete without some collections of poetry and stories. Among the many available are the excellent volumes listed at the close of this chapter. As the teacher discovers poems and stories suited to special occasions and uses, she will find it desirable to make them available for use from year to year. Making a classified list of poems and stories, with references to sources, is one way of doing this. A still better device is to keep a classified file drawer containing cards or sheets of paper on which stories and poems for specific occasions are written or typed. Such a device will enable the teacher to select the right poem for any occasion at a moment's notice. A looseleaf scrapbook is another means.

MEMORIZATION

There should probably be no definite attempt to have children in the first and second grades memorize poetry. However, their impressionable minds will absorb much verse as they hear again and again any poem they enjoy. In no time at all, the children will be joining in as the teacher reads such poems as Muriel Sipe's "Good Morning" or Louise Bechtel's "Grandfather Frog." The latter, with its amusing account of the constant activity of Mr. Frog, will appeal to the sense of humor and the dramatic sense of older children who have recently journeyed to a pond for frog eggs, and they will enjoy repeating the words as the teacher reads aloud. Similarly, they will tend to join in on Lenora Link's "Holding Hands" after hearing it as part of their unit on zoo animals. Memorization thus takes place without effort or real intention.

Communication in a Constructional Activities Period

Some teachers fail to realize the importance of a truly vital feature of the language arts curriculum—the conversation among children as they busy themselves with the crafts, art work, and constructional activities of the modern curriculum. Unless most of the children are engaged in a "quiet" activity such as writing creatively or personal reading, they should feel free to talk quietly as they work. True, they should show self-control and a disposition to be orderly, but subdued, purposeful, friendly conversation and discussion during periods of physical activity should be not only permitted but encouraged.

Learning through units involves much activity by the children. In the process of participating they should talk over quietly the next steps in carrying out the group plans, and the advisable solutions for the problems related to the use of equipment. For instance, several children may be developing a mural portraying modern modes of transportation, while others are arranging a bulletin board display of cut-out pictures of space travel. Still others may be assembling models of planes to be used on the display table. Such constructional activities and handling of audio-visual materials offer opportunities for planning an on-going evaluation of learning activities and materials. Throughout such activities, the children are required to *think* and be resourceful and are developing abilities that will enable them to make independent decisions later on.

Creating a mural not only develops self-expression, but leads to purposeful use of language as children share ideas and work out problems on a common project.

VALUES FOR LANGUAGE IMPROVEMENT

The teacher who knows how to keep all her children quietly convers-
ing or discussing topics of interest while they are busy with their hands
gains rich dividends in language improvement. She learns much about
the established and developing interests of her children. Their grasp
of the sentence, the breadth or poverty of their vocabulary, the presence of speech difficulties or of gross errors in word usage, and their
social as well as emotional adjustment are all revealed as she moves
from group to group. It is an ideal time for her to observe and determine their needs for enrichment or improvement in basic speech
skills such as enunciation. It is a real opportunity for her to know her
children better and to learn how to utilize their interests and meet
their language needs.

In addition, one of the greatest values of the informal communication that takes place during constructional activities is the truly social-
izing influence it exerts. Children constantly offer one another helpful
suggestions; they give and take directions or offer and accept assistance
in the interest of improving their project. Plans that have resulted from
whole-group discussion are found wanting and are modified through
person-to-person exchange of ideas. Eventually, the modifications are
reported back to the class, whose members make evaluations and suggest subsequent procedures. Social adjustments result as certain pupils
shed their shyness and others restrain their excessive aggressiveness.
Their oral expression is natural, informal, and meaningful.

ATTENTION TO SKILLS

In informal types of oral communication that constitute spontaneous
expression, the child is engrossed in the ideas he is expressing, and he
may consequently have little regard for the forms and technicalities of
language. Even so, the fluency and purposefulness in such expression
are desirable goals of language instruction, and they are likely to be
effective.

Within such an informal expressional period the teacher does little to
improve the form of expression except through providing additional
information, suggesting appropriate vocabulary, and being a good example by using a direct manner, clear enunciation, and clear-cut sentence structure. It is through imitating the teacher's effective use of

language that much of the improvement in children's oral expression comes.

Selected References

ANNOTATED BOOK LISTS

A Bibliography of Books for Children. Association for Childhood Education International, 1200 Fifteenth Street, N.W., Washington 5, D.C.

A Rightful Heritage. Landmarks in Children's Literature for the Home Bookshelf, Carnegie Library of Pittsburgh, Pittsburgh, Pennsylvania.

Bibliographical Booklet: Favorite Authors for Boys and Girls. New York: Thomas Y. Crowell Company.

Childrens Books 1964. Children's Book Section, Library of Congress Laboratory. Office of Education, Department of Health and Welfare, Washington, D.C.

Children's Books Too Good to Miss. Western Reserve University, 1133 Bellflower Road, Cleveland, Ohio.

Children's Literature Old and New, V. M. Reid, editor. National Council of Teachers of English, 508 South Sixth Street, Champaign, Illinois.

100 Best Books for Children. McCall's Magazine, 230 Park Avenue, New York 17, New York.

Seven Stories High. Chicago: F. E. Compton & Co.

ANTHOLOGIES OF CHILDREN'S LITERATURE

A Book of Children's Literature. Edited by Lillian Hollowell. New York: Holt, Rinehart & Winston, Inc., 1950.

Anthology of Children's Literature. Compiled by May Hill Arbuthnot. (Includes *Time for Poetry* in following list). Chicago: Scott, Foresman & Co., 1961.

Anthology of Children's Literature. Compiled by Edna Johnson, *et al.* Boston: Houghton Mifflin Co., 1960.

Children and Books. Compiled by May Hill Arbuthnot. Chicago: Scott, Foresman & Co., 1964.

Story and Verse for Children. Edited by Miriam Blanton Huber. New York: The Macmillan Co., 1955.

ANTHOLOGIES OF POETRY

A Small Child's Book of Verse. Compiled by Pelagie Doane. New York: Oxford University Press, 1948.

A *Treasury of Verse for Little Children.* Compiled by M. G. Edgar. New York: Thomas Y. Crowell Co.

An *Inheritance of Poetry.* Compiled by Gladys Adshead and Annis Duff. Boston: Houghton Mifflin Co., 1948.

Bridled with Rainbows. Compiled by Sara and John E. Brewton. (See also *Gaily We Parade* and *Under the Tent Sky*). New York: The Macmillan Co., 1950.

Find Time for Poetry. Compiled by Gretchen Wulfing. Curriculum Guide 1960, Oakland Public Schools, Oakland, California.

For a Child: Great Poems Old and New. Edited by Wilma McFarland. Philadelphia: Westminster Press, 1947.

Let's Enjoy Poetry. Compiled by Rosalind Hughes. Boston: Houghton Mifflin Co., 1961.

My Poetry Book. Compiled by G. T. Huffard and others. New York: Holt, Rinehart & Winston, Inc., 1956.

One Thousand Poems for Children. Edited by Elizabeth Sechrist. Philadelphia: Macrae Smith Co., 1946.

Rainbow in the Sky. Edited by Louis Untermeyer. New York: Harcourt, Brace & World, Inc., 1935.

Sing a Song of Seasons. Compiled by Sara and John E. Brewton. New York: The Macmillan Co., 1955.

Sung Under the Silver Umbrella and *Sung Under the Blue Umbrella.* Selected by the Literature Committee of the Association for Childhood Education International. New York: The Macmillan Co., 1956.

The Cherry Tree. Selected by Geoffrey Grigson. New York: Vanguard Press, Inc., 1962.

The Golden Flute: An Anthology of Poetry for Young Children. Compiled by Alice Hubbard and Adeline Babbitt. New York: John Day Co., 1932.

The Golden Treasury of Poetry. Edited by Louis Untermeyer. New York: Golden Press, Inc., 1959.

Time for Poetry. Compiled by May Hill Arbuthnot. Chicago: Scott, Foresman & Co., 1961.

BOOKS OF VERSE AND SONG

SING IT, SAY IT, OR READ IT

ALDIS, DOROTHY. *All Together.* New York: G. P. Putnam's Sons, 1952.

BARROWS, MARJORIE. *Two Hundred Best Poems for Boys and Girls.* New York: Grosset & Dunlap, Inc., 1942.

BEHN, HARRY. *The Little Hill.* New York: Harcourt, Brace & World, Inc., 1949.

————. *Windy Morning.* New York: Harcourt, Brace & World, Inc., 1953.

CHASE, RICHARD. *Hullabaloo and Other Singing Games*. Boston: Houghton Mifflin Co.

CHUTE, MARCHETTE. *Rhymes About the City* and *Rhymes About the Country*. New York: The Macmillan Co., 1946 and 1941.

COATSWORTH, ELIZABETH. *Summer Green*. New York: The Macmillan Co.

DE LA MARE, WALTER. *Rhymes and Verses: Collected Poems for Children*. New York: Holt, Rinehart & Winston, Inc., 1947.

FARJEON, ELEANOR. *Poetry for Children*. Philadelphia: J. B. Lippincott Co., 1951.

FIELD, RACHEL. *Taxis and Toadstools*. New York: Doubleday & Co., Inc., 1926.

FROST, FRANCES. *The Little Whistler*. New York: Whittlesey House (Mc-Graw-Hill), 1949.

LEAR, EDWARD. *Complete Nonsense Book*. Edited by Lady Strachey. New York: Dodd, Mead & Co. (accelerated group)

MC EWEN, CATHERINE SCHAERRER. *Away We Go!* (One Hundred Poems for the Very Young). New York: Thomas Y. Crowell Co., 1956.

MILNE, A. A. *New We Are Six* and *When We Were Very Young*. New York: E. P. Dutton & Co., 1961.

PETERSHAM, MAUD AND MISKA. *The Rooster Crows*. New York: The Macmillan Co., 1945.

RICHARDS, LAURA. *Tirra Lirra, Rhymes Old and New*. Boston: Little, Brown & Co., 1955.

ROBERTS, ELIZABETH MADDOX. *Under the Tree*. New York: Viking Press, 1922.

ROBINSON, TOM. *In and Out*. New York: Viking Press, 1943.

TIPPETT, J. S. *I Go A Traveling; I Live in a City; I Know Some Animals*. New York: Harper & Brothers, 1929, 1927, and 1941.

SEEGER, RUTH CRAWFORD. *American Folk Songs for Children*. New York: Doubleday & Co., Inc., 1948.

BOOKS EVERY CHILD SHOULD KNOW

ADELSON, LEONE. *The Blowaway Hat*. New York: David McKay Co., Inc.

ANGLUND, JOAN WALSH. *A Friend Is Someone Who Likes You*. New York: Harcourt, Brace & World, Inc., 1958.

———. *Nibble, Nibble, Mousekin*. New York: Harcourt, Brace & World, Inc., 1962.

BANNON, LAURA. *Little People of the Night*. Boston: Houghton Mifflin Co., 1963.

BECKER, CHARLOTTE. *Three Little Steps*. New York: Charles Scribner's Sons.

BENNETT, RICHARD. *Not A Teeny Weeny Wink.* New York: Doubleday & Co., Inc., 1959.

BERTAIL, INEZ. *Time For Bed.* New York: Doubleday & Co., Inc., 1961.

BLEGVAT, LENORE. *Mr. Jensen and Cat.* Harcourt, Brace & World, Inc., 1965.

BRANLEY, FRANKLYN M. *Flash, Crash, Rumble and Roll.* New York: Thomas Y. Crowell Co., 1964.

BROWN, MARCIA, editor. *Three Billy Goats Gruff.* New York: Harcourt, Brace & World, Inc., 1957.

BUCK, PEARL S. *Big Wave.* New York: John Day Co., 1948.

BURTON, VIRGINIA LEE. *Mike Mulligan and His Steam Shovel.* Boston: Houghton Mifflin Co.

COLMAN, HILA. *Peter's Brownstone House.* New York: William Morrow and Co., Inc., 1963.

FLACK, MARJORIE. *Walter the Lazy Mouse.* New York: Doubleday & Co., Inc., 1963.

FLORA, JAMES. *Grandpa's Farm.* New York: Harcourt, Brace & World, Inc., 1965.

GÁG, WANDA. *Gone Is Gone.* New York: Coward-McCann, Inc., 1939.

———. *Millions of Cats.* New York: Coward-McCann, Inc., 1928.

GRAMATKY, HARDIE. *Little Toot.* New York: G. P. Putnam's Sons, 1939.

———. *Little Toot of the Thames.* New York: G. P. Putnam's Sons, 1964.

———. *Loopy.* New York: G. P. Putnam's Sons, 1941.

KEATS, EZRA JACK. *The Snowy Day.* New York: Viking Press, 1962.

KEY, ALEXANDER SPROCKETS. *A Little Robot.* Philadelphia: Westminster Press, 1963. (accelerated groups)

LIONNI, LEO. *Swimmy.* New York: Pantheon Books, Inc., 1963.

LIVINGSTON, MYRA. *I'm Not Me.* New York: Harcourt, Brace & World, Inc., 1963.

MILNE, A. A. *The House at Pooh Corner.* New York: E. P. Dutton & Co., 1961.

———. *Winnie the Pooh.* New York: E. P. Dutton & Co., 1961.

PLASMATI, VALDINE. *Algernon and the Pigeons.* New York: Viking Press, 1963.

POLITI, LEO. *Piccolo's Prank.* New York: Charles Scribner's Sons, 1965.

REY, HANS A. *Curious George.* Boston: Houghton Mifflin Co., 1941.

———. *Curious George Learns the Alphabet.* Boston: Houghton Mifflin Co., 1963.

SCOTT, SALLY. *Jenny and the Wonderful Jeep.* New York: Harcourt, Brace & World, Inc., 1963.

SENDAK, MAURICE. *Where the Wild Things Are.* New York: Harper & Row Publishers, 1963.

SEUSS, DR. (Theodore Seuss Geisel). *Hop on Pop.* New York: Random House, 1963.

——. *And to Think That I Saw It on Mulberry St.* New York: Vanguard Press.

SHALLENBERGER, ALICE. *Little High Hill.* San Carlos, California: Golden Gate Junior Books, 1965.

THALER, MIKE. *Penny Pencil.* New York: Harper & Row Publishers, 1963.

UNWIN, NORA S. *Proud Pumpkin.* New York: E. P. Dutton & Co., 1953.

WONDRISKA, WILLIAM. *A Long Piece of String.* New York: Holt, Rinehart & Winston, Inc., 1963.

ZOLOTOW, CHARLOTTE. *Do You Know What I'll Do?* New York: Harper & Row Publishers, 1958.

BOOKS ABOUT CHILDREN OF OTHER LANDS

BACMEISTER, RHODA. *The People Downstairs and Other Stories.* New York: Coward-McCann, Inc., 1964.

BANNON, LAURA. *Manuela's Birthday in Old Mexico.* Chicago: Albert Whitman & Co., 1939.

BUCK, PEARL S. *The Chinese Children Next Door.* New York: John Day Co., Inc., 1942.

——. *Welcome Child.* New York: John Day Co., Inc., 1964.

ETS, MARIE H. *Gilberto and the Wind.* New York: Viking Press, 1963.

EVANS, RUTH. *The Jungle of Tonza Mara.* New York: The Macmillan Co., 1963. (accelerated groups)

HEIN, JANE HARMON. *Un Jour A La Foire* (translation added). New York: Viking Press, 1963.

JUSTUS, MAY. *New Boy in School.* New York: Hastings House Publishers, Inc., 1963.

LINDGREN, ASTRID. *Marko Lives in Yugoslavia.* New York: The Macmillan Co.

SWENSON, JULIET MORGAN. *Hawaii: A Book to Begin On.* New York: Holt, Rinehart & Winston, Inc., 1963.

YASHIMA, TARO. *Crow Boy.* New York: Viking Press, 1955.

——. *The Village Tree.* New York: Viking Press, 1953.

BOOKS FOR INFORMATION

BARR, JENE. *Baker Bill.* Racine, Wisconsin: Whitman Publishing Co., 1953.

——. *Fireman Fred.* Racine, Wisconsin: Whitman Publishing Co., 1952.

BATE, NORMAN. *Who Fishes for Oil?* New York: Charles Scribner's Sons, 1955.

BRANLEY, FRANKLYN M. *A Book of Moon Rockets for You.* New York: Thomas Y. Crowell Co., 1959. (accelerated groups)

————. *A Book of Astronauts for You*. New York: Thomas Y. Crowell Co., 1963. (accelerated groups)

————. *What the Moon is Like*. New York: Thomas Y. Crowell Co., 1963.

CHARLES, NICHOLAS. *How Do You Get From Here to There?* New York: The Macmillan Co., 1962.

COLONIUS, LILLIAN. *At the Library*. Chicago: Melmont Publishing Co. (a subsidiary of Children's Press, 301 South Racine Avenue, Chicago 17, Illinois).

FRANÇOISE. *What Time Is It, Jeanne-Marie?* New York: Charles Scribner's Sons, 1963.

GANS, ROMA. *Icebergs*. New York: Thomas Y. Crowell Co., 1964.

GOLDIN, AUGUSTA. *Spider Silk*. New York: Thomas Y. Crowell Co., 1964.

GRAMATKY, HARDIE. *Hercules: The Story of the Old-Fashioned Fire Engine*. New York: G. P. Putnam's Sons, 1940.

HAMILTON, LEE DAVID. *Adventures with Elsie the Famous Cow*. New York: G. P. Putnam's Sons, 1964.

JERVIS, DEREK and BEALES, JOAN. *The Seasons*. New York: John Day Co., Inc., 1963.

KUMIN, MAXINE. *Follow the Fall*. New York: G. P. Putnam's Sons, 1961.

————. *Spring Things*. New York: G. P. Putnam's Sons, 1961.

————. *Summer Story*. New York: G. P. Putnam's Sons, 1961.

LENSKI, LOIS. *We Live in the City*. Philadelphia: J. B. Lippincott Co., 1954.

LENT, HENRY. *Diggers and Builders*. New York: The Macmillan Co., 1931.

MOORE, LILIAN and FIAMMENGHI, GIOIA. *Little Racoon and the Thing in the Pool*. New York: McGraw-Hill Book Co., Inc., 1963.

PALAZZO, TONY. *A Pig For Tom*. Edited by Elizabeth M. Graves. Champaign, Illinois: Garrard Press, 1963.

SCHWARTZ, JULIUS. *The Earth Is Your Spaceship*. New York: Whittlesey House (McGraw-Hill), 1963.

ZOLOTOW, CHARLOTTE. *The Sky Was Blue*. New York: Harper & Row Publishers, 1963.

MISCELLANEOUS

GREEN, ROGER LANCELYN. *Authors and Places*. New York: G. P. Putnam's Sons, 1964. (Boys and girls in accelerated groups may use this to find out about authors and the places that inspired them.)

HUTCHINSON, VERONICA. *Chimney Corner Stories*. New York: G. P. Putnam's Sons, 1925.

KASE, ROBERT. *Stories for Creative Acting*. Publisher: Samuel French, 7623 Sunset Boulevard, Hollywood, California. (stories recommended and used successfully by leading creative dramatics directors and teachers)

SIKS, GERALDINE BRAIN. *Children's Literature for Dramatization*. Evanston, Illinois: Harper & Row Publishers, 1964. (teacher's use)

BOOKS FOR THE TEACHER TO KNOW

ARBUTHNOT, MAY HILL. *Time For Fairy Tales*. Chicago: Scott, Foresman & Co., 1952.

BETT, HENRY. *Nursery Rhymes and Tales*. New York: Holt, Rinehart & Winston, Inc.

BREWTON, JOHN E. and SARA. *Index to Children's Poetry*. New York: H. W. Wilson Co., 1942 (first supplement 1954).

FERRIS, HELEN. *Writing Books for Boys and Girls*. New York: Doubleday & Co., Inc.

HARRIS, JOEL CHANDLER. *The Favorite Uncle Remus*. Boston: Houghton Mifflin Co.

HERSHOLT, JEAN, translator. *The Complete Hans Andersen*. Heritage Press, 1949.

HUNT, MARGARET, translator. *Grimm's Fairy Tales*. New York: Pantheon Books, Inc., 1944.

JACOBS, JOSEPH, editor. *The Fables of Aesop*. New York: The Macmillan Co., 1950.

KIPLING, RUDYARD. *Just So Stories*. New York: Doubleday & Co., Inc., 1952.

SANDBURG, CARL. *The Rootabaga Stories*. New York: Harcourt, Brace & World, Inc., 1951.

WIGGIN, KATE DOUGLAS, editor. *Arabian Nights: Their Best Known Tales*. New York: Charles Scribner's Sons, 1909.

SUGGESTED READINGS

BAMMAN, A. H., *et al*. *Oral Interpretation of Children's Literature*, Chapters 3, 4. Dubuque, Iowa: William C. Brown Co., 1964.

COMMISSION ON THE ENGLISH CURRICULUM. *Language Arts for Today's Children*, Chapter 5. New York: Appleton-Century-Crofts, Inc., 1954.

DAWSON, MILDRED, *et al*. *Guiding Language Learning*, Chapter 11. New York: Harcourt, Brace & World, Inc., 1963.

MACKINTOSH, HELEN, editor. *Children and Oral Language*, pp. 21–24; 34–35. National Council of Teachers of English, 1964.

SHANE, HAROLD, *et al*. *Improving Language Arts Instruction in the Elementary School*, pp. 404–13. Columbus, Ohio: Charles Merrill Books, Inc., 1962.

STRICKLAND, RUTH G. *Language Arts in the Elementary School*, Chapter 7. Boston: D. C. Heath & Co., 1957.

Costumes and props help children to react more readily and talk more freely as they prepare a dramatization for formal presentation.

5

The More Organized Forms of Oral Communication

THE ORGANIZED forms of oral communication involve planning—a thinking through of what is to be said so that it may be clear, interesting, properly sequential, and appropriate. The speaker should have certain standards in mind, such as sticking to the point, arranging ideas in good order, or using vivid words. In general, such preplanned speaking is more appropriate in second grade than in kindergarten or first grade. However, younger children of unusual maturity and superior ability may be ready to prepare an orderly presentation of ideas, and, indeed, be desirous of doing so. Any child of any age who manifests readiness for such communication should be encouraged to plan and present his story or report in a somewhat formalized fashion.

These more organized forms of communication include storytelling (but not brief accounts of personal experiences), explanations and directions, reporting, discussion of a problem after considerable time devoted to thinking through likely solutions, dramatization thoughtfully prepared for later presentation, and choral speaking of a type calling for practice and rehearsal. Speaking in such situations is not "off the cuff."

The Group Story

The first-grade teacher usually needs to give constant guidance as the children discuss an experience and then organize their ideas into a group story which she records on the chalkboard or a pencil pad. After encouraging wide participation and drawing forth all possible viewpoints, she helps the children to formulate and select sentences that best express the thoughts and to arrange them in desirable sequence. They thus work toward a simple, clear-cut, orderly presentation.

The more advanced first-grade children develop the ability to write a few sentences independently, though they may require preliminary oral discussion in order to organize their thoughts. Many second-grade children will have developed this ability. Group stories planned by younger children and dictated to the teacher, as well as the first ones written independently by individuals, will be rather short and expressed in brief sentences, such as the story that follows:

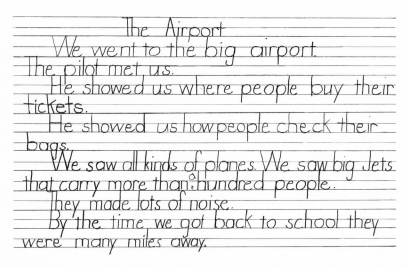

The Airport
We went to the big airport.
The pilot met us.
He showed us where people buy their tickets.
He showed us how people check their bags.
We saw all kinds of planes. We saw big Jets that carry more than a hundred people.
They made lots of noise.
By the time we got back to school they were many miles away.

First graders were excited after visiting the airport and seeing jet aircraft take off for faraway places. After talking over the interesting things they saw, class members dictated the above story to the teacher. It reflects an orderly account of the class trip.

The more mature children can take considerable responsibility for deciding what facts and ideas to include and for determining the proper sequential order in the story. Prior to any dictation or independent writing, the group will engage in thoughtful, organized discussion; that is, they will plan and work toward definite ends.

PLANNING THROUGH ORDERLY DISCUSSION

Note in the discussion that follows how the teacher guides the children in developing an orderly presentation of their group story about a trip to see a sleeping car. In doing so, she secures a variety of suggested sentences and then helps the children to choose the more clearly expressed ideas and to arrange them in correct sequence.

SUE. Miss Lane, may we write a story about our visit to the train? I would like to put the story in my train book.

BILLY. Oh, yes. May we, Miss Lane? I'd like to read our story to Father and Mother.

MISS LANE. Sue and Billy have a good idea, haven't they? If you will all think hard about what you wish to say, I'll write your story on the board. What title do you want to use for the story?

JIMMY. We Visit a Train.

MISS LANE. Do you all like that title? (*The children agree that they do, and Miss Lane writes the title on the board.*) Now, what do you want to say first? What will your first sentence be? (*Several sentences are suggested, but they are not accepted by the class.*)

SUE. Friday morning we went to visit a train. (*This sentence is accepted by the class, and Miss Lane writes it.*)

MISS LANE. What will your next sentence be?

JIMMY (*after several others have suggested sentences*). It was standing on a sidetrack. (*The class accepts this sentence.*)

MISS LANE. What next? How did the train happen to be on the sidetrack? (*After various suggestions, the following sentences are accepted by the class.*)

TED. The train stays there all day.

BILLY. Some men get it ready for the next night trip.

ANNE. It must be ready to leave at four o'clock. (*And so the story goes on.*)

SPECIFIC VALUES IN TERMS OF LANGUAGE ABILITY

It is obvious that the writing of a cooperative story of this kind calls, first of all, for thoughtful oral expression. It will involve such experiences in thinking and expression as:

Deciding which events or ideas to include
Determining the correct sequence of events or ideas
Building a sentence to express each thought
Choosing the exact words to convey the thought
Using correct word forms

The cooperative story thus develops orderly thinking and discussion and also entails language values that will function in independent story writing later.

In addition, when the children copy the story, there will be concentration on writing skills including capitalization, punctuation, and spelling. It is important that, from the beginning of practical writing, children try to use such mechanics correctly. The cooperative story promotes such learnings when the teacher, as she writes the sentences on the board, frequently calls attention to the end punctuation for sentences and to the use of capital letters wherever they are needed.

Interpreting and Giving Directions

In the modern classroom program, there are many occasions for the children to receive and interpret directions, instructions, and explanations, and to give them to classmates as well. To be effective, these types of communication must be well organized. Planning ahead of time is essential.

LISTENING TO AND FOLLOWING DIRECTIONS

Experiences in listening to, interpreting, and following directions may be provided at almost any period in the day if the teacher is alert to the opportunity and uses it to advance language training. Children love to assist the teacher, and they are only too glad to be called upon for such assistance as is indicated by the directions that follow:

"John, please open the top right-hand drawer in my desk. Find the green notebook and bring it to me."

"Beth, please go to the bookcase. Find the six copies of *Here and There with Henry*. Then pass them out to the reading group."

Such directions, *given only once,* accustom the children to attentive listening and thoughtful interpretation. Should John or Beth fail to pass the test of attention and interpretation, the teacher should ask another child to follow the directions. But she should seek an early opportunity to put John or Beth to similar tests until the child is able to listen, interpret, and execute correctly at a single telling—an ability that is based on good listening and organized thinking. As reading ability develops, simple directions may be written on the board.

All too often the busy teacher tends to do too much herself and fails to seize opportunities to develop good listening habits, self-reliance, and a sense of real responsibility on the part of children. She perhaps overassists a child to whom she has given a particular job, repeats directions several times, or assigns jobs only to those pupils who have already demonstrated their ability to take directions. Since her task is to help all the children learn, she should seize every opportunity to advance each pupil's skills in taking and following directions accurately. In harmony with the conception of the language arts program as a daylong activity, the teacher must look upon every opportunity for communication as a feature of that program and therefore utilize the giving of directions, instructions, and explanations, both by herself and by the children, as opportunities for increasing the children's ability to listen, to interpret, to think, and to express.

LEARNING TO GIVE DIRECTIONS

If a child's instructions, directions, or explanations are to be clear, he must be thoroughly familiar with an object or process with which he is concerned. For instance, he should be able to demonstrate how to hold a saw if he is explaining how to keep the implement from being "balky."

The child must learn to keep his listeners in mind when planning and giving instructions or directions. For instance, when he is trying to tell a new teacher how to reach his home for a call upon his mother, he has to be very exact. He must know the names of streets, the number of blocks to go in each successive direction, and the location of key buildings or stoplights that may act as guideposts along the way. If he bungles in his first effort to give his teacher the correct directions, the teacher may suggest that he start anew after thinking through a clear-cut set of directions.

After observing his father plant some bulbs, the child may take the responsibility of telling classmates how to make plantings in preparation for Mother's Day, when the children may wish to take a potted plant home. Again, he must plan how to instruct his fellow students; he must speak in sentences that clearly convey his meaning; and the sentences must be in the right order.

It is not easy to give instructions, directions, or explanations—not even for the teacher or for any other adult. Doing so in a satisfactory way calls for careful planning. Children gladly accept the challenge to be effective in these types of communication when there is something to be accomplished through engaging in them. Granted a worthwhile end and the chance to be thoroughly familiar with a process, a child can do a good job.

Reports on Observations

In first or second grade, a report is usually informal. For example, one child may have watched a zoo attendant feed the seals, and he describes the scene in detail so that his classmates can visualize what he watched.

Another may have watched a group of workers near his home paving a side street, and he explains the process or procedure he has observed to his interested audience (who may thus be stimulated to plan a trip to see these same street workers).

In general, there is less giving of individual reports in kindergarten or first grade than in second grade.

DIRECTED OBSERVATIONS

In presenting such a report, there is a demand for a certain degree of organization of materials. However, the organization will grow out of the nature of the topic or experience upon which the report is based. In reporting on a bird, for example, the child should sense the need for describing color, size, song or call, actions or nest-building technique, location of the bird, and other distinguishing characteristics or

A child's personal experience might be the basis for a class report such as this one on horses where pictures and a carefully prepared written story have been assembled for the presentation.

facts, if he wishes his hearers to identify the bird from his description.

To develop the children's sense of organization, the teacher will plan special periods for observation, sometimes of objects or pets brought into the classroom and sometimes through observation trips outdoors. In preparation, she will raise questions designed to direct the children's observation, or stimulate the group to raise them. On a first trip to observe spring birds, the group may be directed in discussing what to look for and in listing questions like the following:

> What color is the bird?
> Is he as big as a robin?
> What is he doing?
> What kind of song or call has he?
> What kind of nest is he building?

If children are to observe (study) an abandoned oriole's nest brought into the classroom in the fall, questions like the following may be raised:

> What is the nest made of?
> How are the materials put together?
> What size is it? What shape is it?
> What bird builds this kind of nest?

When the children grow accustomed to organized observation, they will develop the habit of organized reporting.

THE INDIVIDUAL REPORT

By the second half of the year, a second-grade child should plan an occasional individual report. Perhaps he is to tell about the progress of his committee in carrying out an enterprise assigned to them by the class. He will probably organize his report in terms of the sequence of the committee's activities and conclude with a statement of things still to be accomplished. Sometimes a child may report on an out-of-school experience. Again, he is likely to organize his report according to sequence. In fact, the main type of organization that may be expected of young children will be the sequential type.

A girl in the second grade had just returned from a winter in Florida. One of her most exciting experiences had been the opportunity to sleep in an upper berth. Upon her mention of this fact, her classmates asked her to tell all about it, or to "make a report." This is what the child said about her experience:

> On the train I slept in an upper berth. I watched the porter make it up. First he pulled down a shelf that was up against the ceiling of the coach. It had pillows and blankets on it. He used some of these to make Mother's bed in the lower berth. The others he used to make my bed. When the bed was ready, the porter brought a little ladder and I climbed up. It was fun to sleep so high up.

Discussion Toward Specific Ends

The discussion that precedes a reading lesson or that occurs during the oral exchange of news items may be quite informal. Often it is really more like conversation than discussion. The contrary is true when a group is discussing definite plans for carrying on some activity.

PLANNING A GROUP ENTERPRISE

In planning a trip to visit a dairy farm, for example, the discussion must be pointed toward definite ends. The procedure in the second grade might be as follows:

> TEACHER (*raising questions to stimulate thought and discussion*). If we wish to visit Mr. Lane's dairy farm, what plans must we make? (*Children make various suggestions.*)
>
> JIMMY. I think we ought to make a list of things we have to do.

The class accepts Jimmy's suggestion and proceeds to discuss ways and means. The following list, dictated (under teacher guidance) by the children and written on the board by the teacher, is a written language outcome of the discussion:

Plans for Our Trip

1. Write a note to our principal asking permission to visit the dairy farm.
2. Write a class note to Mr. Lane to find out when we may visit his farm.
3. Find out which fathers or mothers will take us and bring us back.
4. List questions to ask Mr. Lane at his farm.
5. Divide the questions among us.
6. Make some safety rules for the trip.
7. Make some courtesy rules.

Then there follows some discussion of each of the items, the teacher suggesting it as follows:

> TEACHER. Now that we have our list of what we must do, which point must we discuss first?

LANGUAGE VALUES

Naturally, only part of the listed points will be handled in one period. Item 1 would probably be the first point, and discussing and composing the note will occupy an entire written-language period. Copying it may occupy another. Most of the other steps in planning will require a period or more.

Organized discussion of the kind indicated above provides definite training in discussion and in organization of ideas in that it requires the child to:

1. Think about a definite point and stick to it in discussion
2. Feel responsible for contributing to the discussion
3. Contribute something of value whenever he speaks
4. State his ideas clearly if he expects them to be considered by the group
5. Listen thoughtfully to each speaker
6. Take his turn, and not monopolize

BY-PRODUCTS IN OTHER TYPES OF EXPRESSION

Notice the many language by-products in opportunities for further expressional work to be carried on in later periods: (1) planning, dictating, and copying a class note; (2) planning and copying a class letter; (3) discussing and listing questions to guide observation; (4) discussing, composing, and listing safety and courtesy rules. Also, observe (5) that the concept of the sentence (the *complete thought* idea) is strengthened by such activities as composing sentences for the note and the letter and listing plans, questions, or rules; (6) that the teacher's writing of the children's sentences on the board reviews again and again the correct form for writing statements, commands, and questions; and (7) that the children receive practice in capitalization, punctuation, spelling, and writing while copying notes, letters, and rules from the board—practice valuable beyond anything routine drill can provide.

Dramatization or Storytelling for an Assembly

Informal storytelling and the dramatization of stories call for originality and spontaneity. Therefore, even in Grade Two informal presentation should receive greater emphasis than the more formal type that involves preplanning in considerable detail and rehearsing before presentation. However, before the end of the second grade, the more advanced pupils should have had experience in presenting a planned and rehearsed play or story in an assembly or some other formal program. Such a presentation calls for careful diction and articulation, clarity of tone, ease of manner, and other qualities of finished, public presentation. In life outside school, there are occasional demands for public appearances of children in connection with religious, community, and social organizations. There should, therefore, be some attention to special-occasion appearances in the language arts curriculum of the school. The preparation of a play or a story for an assembly affords such experience.

PLANNED DRAMATIZATION

A planned dramatization may be discussed in detail and rehearsed until it becomes a finished product. In planning the play, several or all of the following steps should be worked out through discussion:

Several children may take part in gathering and presenting a story report such as this one on Lincoln.

1. Divide the story into scenes or acts, and name each part.
2. List the characters in each act or each scene.
3. Discuss time, place, and setting in connection with each scene or act.
4. Determine the scenery, action, and probable conversation for the first scene or act.
5. Choose a cast for the first tryout.
6. After the tryout, let the group give constructive suggestions and choose another cast for a second tryout.
7. Repeat steps 4, 5, and 6 for each scene of the play.
8. Let the group choose the final cast.
9. Discuss costuming, scenery, and properties in connection with each scene or act. Choose committees to be responsible for preparing or securing whatever is necessary.

There are degrees of formality, and almost any of the steps above may be omitted. Some may be unnecessary; others may seem too restrictive and time-demanding, especially step 9. Experienced teachers have learned that young children tire of dramatization that is unduly formal in its preparation.

There seems little justification for having children memorize a ready-made play such as may be found in some periodicals and books. It is far more educational for the children to plan their own play from an original story or from a story in their readers or in a storybook. The work of planning gives group experience in organizing ideas as to background and action and in creating dialogue appropriate to characters and action. Such planning also gives opportunity for vital discussion, for thoughtful evaluation, and for careful rereading of the story.

As the children plan their play and try out the various scenes, they are likely to find cause to revise, to iron out impossible situations, and to add intriguing complications. The resourcefulness and originality called for by such revisions constitute one of the main values of using pupil-planned plays rather than those printed in books and magazines.

PLANNED STORYTELLING

Often the story selected for presentation in an assembly will be an account of a group or personal experience—one that is entirely new to the audience. It may sometimes be the retelling of a favorite story from a book, though imaginative children may be encouraged to create a story. In preparation, the storyteller, with the counsel and assistance of teacher and classmates, will be responsible for most of the following steps:

1. Selecting an experience or story that is interesting and full of fast-moving action
2. Thinking through the step-by-step development of the story
3. Planning a beginning that will catch interest and attention
4. Choosing vivid words that will create mental pictures in the listeners' minds
5. Rehearsing the story before classmates to get suggestions for improvement
6. Improving the story until it can be told with ease and fluency

Second-grade children should have little rehearsal. Two or three preliminary tellings before the teacher or the homeroom audience should be enough. Help the child to keep in mind such standards as the following:

How to Tell a Story

1. Speak each word distinctly.
2. Keep sentences apart (do not string them together with and's or so's).
3. Look at the audience.
4. Show interest in your own story.

Occasionally, a second grade will present a simple report at an assembly. It may be an account of a group enterprise, presented by several children, each reporting on a phase of it. The steps in preparing for such a report are similar to those in preparing a story.

Choral Speaking

In the first and second grades, scarcely a day will pass without the teacher's reading a poem or two to her children. Such poems may be suggested by the fact that the circus is opening in the town, by something displayed in the show-and-tell period, by a rainy day, by the first snow, or by the new rabbits in Billy's hutch. Sometimes it will be fun for the group just to listen to a nonsense rhyme or to say some familiar nursery rhymes together.

Almost always, a group of children will have favorite poems for which they ask again and again. Usually, after three or four hearings, they begin to say parts of such poems with the teacher as she repeats the familiar lines. Choral speaking may begin in this manner.

VALUES

In the first and second grades, *group speaking* is probably a more suitable term than *choral speaking*. There should be no attempt to achieve the finished performances associated with the latter term. Instead, the children should say their favorite verses together because they find it fun to do so.

Group speaking makes an important contribution to the social aspect of the language arts program by encouraging group cooperation. Children readily realize that verse speaking is not successful unless every child in the group harmonizes his voice and speech with those of the rest of the group. Furthermore, the timid individual is permitted to feel very much a part of the group and can participate without self-consciousness, such as might attend his individual effort to read or recite a poem, and it is hoped that the habits of speech and voice control developed in his group speaking may carry over into his daily speech.

Furthermore, group speaking makes a strong contribution to reading and literature, which are definitely a part of the language arts program. If group speaking is to be successful, children must (1) understand, mentally as well as emotionally, the thought of the poet's lines; (2) appreciate the connotation and also the music of his words; (3) feel the rhythm of the meter; and (4) enjoy the music of rhyme. The extent to which a child enjoys and appreciates literary qualities in poetry will determine the extent to which he later reads verse with real pleasure.

TYPES OF GROUP SPEAKING

Three types of group speaking are especially appropriate for young children. One is the *refrain* type in which the teacher speaks most of a stanza alone, with the children joining in on a refrain, such as "Dink-ums, dunkums, little gray billy goat." Another easy one is the *line-a-child* or *line-a-group* type in which each line or couplet is spoken by a different pupil or small group. "One, two, buckle my shoe" is a jingle of this type. The third type is the *antiphonal,* in which two groups speak in turn, as when one asks a question and the other gives the answer as in "Pussycat, Pussycat, Where Have You Been?" Dialogue is another type of poem to be spoken antiphonally.

Of all the types of group speaking, *unison* is the most difficult. It is hard to blend many voices smoothly. Therefore, unison speaking is stressed more at the upper grade or high school level. However, because children get so much enjoyment and such fine social experience out of unison speaking of familiar nursery rhymes, the kindergarten-primary teacher may advisedly allow children to say their favorite ones together.

Group speaking using refrains   Young children enjoy rhymes with a refrain, for they like to repeat interesting words several times. This type of poetry is easy to make into group-speaking selections. The children first listen to the rhyme for the story or meaning. Then they listen for the refrain so that they may join in on the third reading, but at the same rate and pitch that the teacher is using. Nursery rhymes afford many such poems. Here are two in which the refrain to be spoken with the teacher is in italics.

> *Hickory, dickory, dock,*
> The mouse ran up the clock.
>   The clock struck one,
>   The mouse ran down,
> *Hickory, dickory, dock.*

> *Hickety, pickety, my black hen,*
> She lays eggs for gentlemen;
> Sometimes nine, sometimes ten,
> *Hickety, pickety, my black hen.*

In case a bit of refrain-type verse is well known by a child, that child may replace the teacher as the speaker of the body of the poem. The rest of the class will chime in on the refrain.

Note that rhymes like the two above call for clear-cut pronunciation of words; for instance, note how many of the words end in *k*. Children whose enunciation is muddy are encouraged to speak more clearly and precisely as they contribute to a clearly spoken effect.

Line-a-child speaking of verse Another enjoyable and very simple kind of group speaking is that in which a single child or a very small group speaks only one line or couplet, and each of several individuals or small groups takes a turn at giving a part of the poem. In the following rhyme, eight lines are thus spoken in turn.

> Bow, wow, says the dog;
> Mew, mew, says the cat;
> Grunt, grunt, says the pig;
> And squeak, says the rat.
> Tu, whu, says the owl;
> Caw, caw, goes the crow;
> Quack, quack, goes the duck;
> And moo, moo, says the cow.

In speaking the poem, the children should be encouraged to imitate the actual sound each animal or bird makes, not merely to say words like "mew, mew." Children have fun doing such imitations.

Group speaking in antiphonal fashion When speaking antiphonally, two groups of kindergarten-primary children take turns in speaking, either in the form of dialogue or of questions and answers. Often the opening lines lead into the dialogue or series of questions and answers, or they may come at the end as "clinchers." Such introductory or closing lines may be spoken in unison, or the teacher or a competent pupil may speak them as a solo. For instance, in the following poem, the opening two lines may be presented as a solo or given in unison before the antiphonal rendition of the dialogue.

> Three little mice sat down to spin,
> Pussy passed by and she peeped in.
>
> "What are you doing, my little men?"
> "We're making coats for gentlemen."
>
> "Shall I come in and bite off your threads?"
> "No, no, Miss Pussy, you'll bite off our heads."

"Oh, no, I'll not. I'll help you spin."
"That may be so, but you don't come in."

The next poem is an example of a question-answer poem. Probably the girls (if girls and boys speak in separate groups) should ask the questions and the boys with their slightly heavier voices give the answers.

"Which is the way to London Town,
To see the King in his golden crown?"
"One foot up and one foot down,
That's the way to London Town."

"What is the way to London Town,
To see the Queen in her silken gown?"
"Left! Right! Left! Right! Up and down,
Soon you'll be in London Town!"

Speaking in unison   As mentioned above, speaking in unison is the most difficult of group speaking in terms of keeping the children's voices together and securing a single harmonious effect. But young children so enjoy saying nursery rhymes and very short poems together that many teachers give a few minutes now and then to unison group speaking. Often the class will repeat a rhyme while one or more classmates pantomime it. "Little Jack Horner" and "Little Miss Muffet" may be used in this way.

The following old rhyme may be spoken by the entire class while they act it out as they stand in a circle.

Here we go up, up, up,
And here we go down, down, downy;
Here we go backwards and forwards,
And here we go round, round, roundy.

FINDING APPROPRIATE POEMS

The teacher will find suitable poems in any anthology of children's poetry. Many school readers offer some poems, and perhaps one or more of them may be adapted to group speaking. For the early, more mechanical stage, exemplified by the rhyme "Getting-Up Time," some of the other nursery rhymes may be used.

For a later stage, in which children are able to sense the mood of the lines, suitable poems may be found in any of the anthologies listed at the close of Chapter 4. Criteria for selection should be: (1) brevity, (2) simplicity of vocabulary and phrasing, (3) marked rhythm, (4) appeal to children in thought and structure, (5) contrast of ideas, and (6) literary quality.

ENDS TO BE SOUGHT

In any work with group speaking, the ends to be sought are:

1. Complete enjoyment on the part of the group
2. Literary appreciation (sensing mood, thought, and picturization)
3. Development of a sense of rhythm and phrasing
4. Ear training through rhyme and rhythm
5. Clear enunciation and correct pronunciation
6. Flexibility in volume, quality, and tone of voice
7. Perfect rapport of the group

Above all, group speaking should not be used as a show feature. It is not primarily intended as a performance before an audience. Special stress should be placed upon group enjoyment. Choral speaking is an ancient folk art, and it was originally performed solely for the pleasure of the performing group. This ancient conception should persist with respect to group speaking by young children in the classroom.

Selected References

CHORAL SPEAKING

ABNEY, LOUISE and ROWE, GRACE. *Choral Speaking Arrangements for the Lower Grades.* Magnolia, Massachusetts: Expression Co., Publishers, 1953.

ARBUTHNOT, MAY HILL. *Children and Books,* Chapter 9. Chicago: Scott, Foresman, and Co., 1957.

BAMMAN, H. A., *et al.* *Oral Interpretation of Children's Literature,* Chapter 3. Dubuque, Iowa: William C. Brown Co., 1964.

DE WITT, MARGUERITE E., *et al.* *Practical Methods in Choral Speaking.* Magnolia, Massachusetts: Expression Co., Publishers.

GULLAN, MARJORIE. *Choral Speaking.* Magnolia, Massachusetts: Expression Co., Publishers, 1930.

SCOTT, LOUISE and THOMPSON, J. J. *Talking Time.* St. Louis: Webster Publishing Co., 1951.

SWANN, MONA. *An Approach to Choral Speech.* Magnolia, Massachusetts: Expression Co., Publishers.

SUGGESTED READINGS

DAWSON, MILDRED and DINGEE, FRIEDA. *Children Learn the Language Arts,* pp. 89–93. Minneapolis: Burgess Publishing Co., 1959.

DAWSON, MILDRED, *et al.* *Guiding Language Learning,* Chapter 11. New York: Harcourt, Brace & World, Inc., 1963.

GREENE, HARRY A. and PETTY, WALTER T. *Developing Language Skills in the Elementary School,* Chapters 5, 10, and 11. Boston: Allyn and Bacon, Inc., 1959.

SHANE, HAROLD, *et al.* *Improving Language Arts Instruction in the Elementary School,* Chapter 11. Columbus, Ohio: Charles Merrill Books, Inc., 1962.

6
Written Expression

TYPICAL SIX-YEAR-OLD children have achieved a reasonable degree of ease and effectiveness in using oral language, but early in the first grade they have little or no ability to write down their ideas by themselves. On the average, their speaking vocabulary is likely to be 6000 words or more and their listening and meaning vocabulary more than triple that; they tend to enunciate and articulate their words quite clearly and correctly; their sentences, while uncomplicated and fairly short, may be compound or complex in structure. In writing, they may have learned at home or in kindergarten to print their own names, but usually they have to dictate captions for pictures and sentences that express their ideas. An older person will write these for them until some time in first grade (or later for slow-developing children) when they have learned enough about manuscript writing and the spelling of common words to write for themselves.

While the language activities in first grade tend to be largely oral, children do have real need for written expression from time to time. This is especially true when they are planning a major enterprise, such as making a school garden. For instance, one class kept the following records which were first written on the chalkboard and then transferred to charts or lists on the bulletin board:

Tools We Need   Jobs for Us

Seeds to Buy   Our Work Committees

Our Friday Story (*what had happened week by week*)

Through motivation and discussion children are led to write independent stories about their experiences.

Since it was late in the school year, the children were able to do some of the writing on the chalkboard and to make copies for the charts and bulletin board entries. By consulting their word boxes, they could manage much of the spelling (see p. 128), though the slower learners in the group continued to copy what they had dictated to the teacher.

Children who come from a barren and possibly illiterate home background or who have had to learn English as a second language after entering school may begin second grade with quite limited ability to write independently. From the beginning of the year, therefore, the second-grade teacher serves as their secretary as long as need be and gradually aids them in acquiring the skills that will enable them to write for themselves. Fortunately, many school systems are now providing compensatory education for underprivileged children so that the kindergarten and first-grade programs, in particular, greatly enrich experiences and give much opportunity for oral language activities that build vocabulary and add to the fluency and clarity of the children's sentences. It is most important that teachers give first consideration to enriching their background and developing situations that stimulate these underprivileged pupils to speak freely and to feel the necessity of putting some of their ideas into writing. As we have stressed above, oral language abilities can develop adequately only as children gain a wealth of concepts and as they talk abundantly about the ideas they have gained. Furthermore, it is only as oral language is well handled that children develop readiness for learning to read and to write. Consequently, wide and rich experiences with opportunities to talk about them are basic; upon such bases as these, the teacher can develop in the pupils such skills as capitalizing and punctuating correctly as sentences are written down, spelling more and more of the commonly used words, improving handwriting, and accurately indicating complete sentences. Ideas come first; skills follow.

Developing Sentence Sense

A child begins to express his ideas in full sentences in his early years, but he acquires the ability to string his words into sentences quite unconsciously as he listens to those about him and imitatively adopts the sentence patterns he hears. To the extent that he hears and imitates

English that is standard, he has the advantage of already using the words and sentence patterns of his teacher and the books he will use in school, and thus he has a head start in learning to read and to write. If he has learned a dialect quite different in word choice and in pronunciation from standard English, his teacher must start where he is and gradually, through reading and telling stories to him and through his continued tendency to imitate the language he hears, build up the language patterns called for in reading schoolbooks and in writing informal but standard English. Luckily, sentence patterns vary little between standard English and the various dialects spoken in various homes—word order being about the same; and a patient, understanding teacher can succeed in familiarizing her pupils sufficiently with standard English to prepare them for learning to read and write quite well.

STRESS ON THE SENTENCE IN READING

It is general practice for children's early reading experiences to be based on their reading of the sentences and stories they have dictated to their teacher. Because such informal reading materials are based on their discussion of their own activities and of sentences in their own words, the reading is sure to have familiar meanings, vocabulary, and sentence patterns; and it is likely to be quite fluent and natural. In the processes of dictating their ideas and later reading them a sentence at a time, the children become familiar with the meaning of *sentence*.

As a child learns to read, his teacher will say, "Who can read the first *sentence?*" or "Which *sentence* tells you the puppy's name?" Thus the child grows in the knowledge (unconsciously, of course) that a sentence may tell something or ask something. He even learns how sentences are set apart, in print or in writing, for he sees that there is a capital letter to tell him where a sentence begins, and that there is some kind of mark to show him the end of the sentence. Otherwise he could not read from his reader or read the group story that the teacher has written on the board or on a chart. When she writes on the board, the teacher should consistently strengthen the pupils' concept of sentence form by frequently calling their attention to the capital letter with which she begins the first word in each sentence of the story they dictate as well as to the period or question mark that she places at the end of a sentence. Thus the teacher helps the children to understand the mechanics of the written or printed sentence.

In the second grade, the teacher will work along these same lines. Questions like the following may be injected without interfering with interest in reading:

> "Here is a new story. The first *sentence* tells where Toni went. Who can read that *sentence?* Which *sentence* tells what Toni found?"
>
> "John, the next *sentence* is a short one. Will you read it to us?"
>
> "Mary, will you read the *long sentence* that comes next?"
>
> "You have just learned the word *elephant.* Can you find two sentences on the next page that have the word *elephant* in them?

Again, in composing a class story, the teacher will ask, "What shall we tell in our *first sentence?*" "Who can suggest the *second sentence?*" and so on. When the story is completed, she may ask, "Isn't this a good, long story? How many sentences did we put in it? How can you tell?"

BUILDING THE SENTENCE CONCEPT

There is no formal sentence analysis in the second grade. If, by the end of the year, the child senses the fact that a sentence tells something, or asks a question, or tells what to do (as in directions or rules), he has grasped the concept of the complete thought.

In both oral and written work, the teacher should strive to eliminate the fault of stringing sentences together with "and," "and-a," "why-a," "so-a," or "then-a." As this fault is eliminated in oral expression, the sentence concept is strengthened, and improvement of the written sentence follows. In connection with a planned story, she may suggest, "When you tell your story, stop and think what you wish to say before you begin each sentence. That will help you to make a better sentence, and it will help us to catch up with what you are telling us."

A time-proven and recently validated way of promoting sentence sense is having the children plan and give three-sentence stories—either orally or in writing. The procedure may begin as follows: the teacher displays pictures of three or four interesting objects or creatures or lists their names on the chalkboard. For instance, she might list these words on the board: *puppy, doll, roller skates, father.* She then says, "Choose one of these. Think of a little story for the one you choose. Think of just three things. Then tell each thing in one sentence. When you tell your story, stop a little at the end of each sentence. I will show you how your story will sound. Listen to see how I stop a little after each sentence.

> "I have a new car.   (*pause*)
> It is a blue Volkswagen.   (*pause*)
> I drove it to school this morning."

The teacher may write her own story on the chalkboard after giving it and then have a child read it a sentence at a time. Some of the children's stories may be similarly put on the board and read. Their conscious planning of just three facts, their telling each fact in a distinctly separate sentence, and their reading it aloud are effective ways of building true sentence sense.

CORRECTIVE WORK

During a period of spontaneous discussion or storytelling, it is inadvisable to call a child's attention to his *and*-fault lest he be discouraged from voluntary participation. A child should never feel repressed or self-conscious in his desires or efforts to speak. Whenever the teacher notices that a child needs help in sentence structure, she may set up a period for telling three-sentence stories in which the children deliberately work at using distinct sentences. A period devoted to spontaneous expression is no time for correction.

Sometimes the teacher may make up a story with *and*-faults similar to those in the children's stories. She may then have the children listen to see what is wrong with her sentences and work together to improve them. Again, each child who states a separate sentence correctly is getting reinforcement of his sentence sense. (The children who need help should be the only ones included in such a lesson.) The children will also enjoy having their three-sentence stories put on tape so they might listen and evaluate their products. Some stories may need some improvement, and the deliberate statement of each sentence as it should be stated as a separate entity will help sentence sense.

Often the *"and-a's"* and *"why-a's"* that pepper a child's story may result from his slow thinking or lack of an idea as to what to say next. As children are directed to observe closely and as they participate in numerous enriching activities and experiences, their ideas will multiply and—with frequent opportunities to express themselves—they will become more fluent and will less frequently tie sentences together with a hesitant *"why-a"* or *"and-a."*

Capitalization and Punctuation

In the first grade, most of the children can and should learn to use capital letters for the following: (1) their own names, (2) names of classmates, (3) names of pets, (4) the word *I*, and (5) the first word in a sentence. Children involved in the language-experience approach to reading (writing and reading their own stories) often will learn such uses of the capital letters early in the first grade. However, children retarded in their learning because of barrenness of experience or very low ability may continue to dictate to the teacher all through first grade and still be able to use capital letters only as they copy their dictated compositions when they enter second grade. Teachers must expect great variation in children's levels of learning in such mechanics as capitalization and punctuation and must expect from each child only as much as he is able to do.

The capitalized items to which second-grade children may at least be introduced are as follows. (The above items for first grade are included again here.)

> The name of a book, city, day, month, person, pet, school, state, street, story
> The word *I*
> The first word in a sentence
> The first word in a line of poetry
> The first word in the greeting and closing of a note or letter
> The title before a person's name and for a picture or poster

The first instruction in using capital letters in the second grade will probably occur in connection with heading papers. The group should be taught at once the prescribed heading for use in the school and grade, and should understand that the heading is to be used for each written lesson. If, in addition to the child's own name (first and last), the date and the name of the school are used in the heading, the use of capital letters for the name of the month and of the school can thus be established and become habitual in connection with a very practical daily need. In a special place on the board, the teacher should write the name of the school (calling attention to capital letters and to spelling), and the date, changing the latter from day to day and month to month. It may be advisable to reserve the writing of the date until the latter part of the year.

In connection with a cooperative note, which the teacher writes on the board, the use of capital letters in the greeting and in the closing will be noted. However, most children need only be instructed to copy these capital letters correctly, since only the more advanced will write a note independently. Each child should also learn how to write his own address, using capital letters correctly for street, town or county, and state. But general rules for the use of capital letters should not be taught.

From time to time, written stories, notes, and notices may call for the writing of other proper names. The use of capital letters in such instances should be pointed out. Yet the general principle of teaching the use of capital letters only in connection with day-to-day practical situations should apply, as rules mean nothing to young children.

In the early grades, the few uses of punctuation marks include the period and question mark for sentence endings and perhaps the period to follow *Mr.* and *Mrs.* These should become habitual by constant use. If the commas after the greeting of a letter, in a date, and in an address are needed, they will usually be copied from the board.

Spelling

As children progress in their developmental reading program, they learn the various skills of word recognition. For instance, they come to recognize the names of the letters of the alphabet and also their sounds, taken singly or in blends and digraphs. They also learn how to analyze a word with respect to its parts, such as; (1) *s* or *es* endings, (2) *ing* and *d* or *ed* endings, and (3) parts of a compound word. These same skills carry over into the ability to attack the spelling of a word. Children, therefore, gradually acquire readiness for spelling instruction as they learn to attack new words in their reading vocabulary independently.

Actually, most children do learn to spell, without conscious effort, the words that they commonly use. They watch the teacher as she writes their news stories and experience stories on the board. They engage in matching exercises in which they must closely inspect word and phrase cards in order to find the corresponding word or phrase in a chart story. They learn to copy announcements and records that the teacher has written down for them. They do seatwork in connection

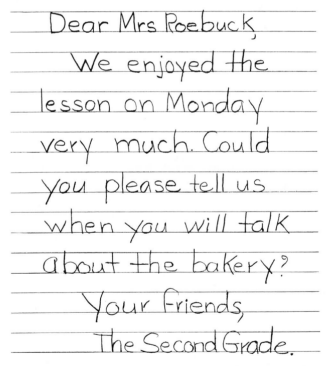

Dear Mrs Roebuck,

We enjoyed the lesson on Monday very much. Could you please tell us when you will talk about the bakery?

Your friends,

The Second Grade.

After watching a yeast experiment on television, the class wrote a letter to the television teacher asking for more information about the bakery. The letter was planned and dictated by the group.

with the development of reading skills in which they write certain words frequently. As a result, such common words as *jump, come, school, home,* and *mother* are learned incidentally—perhaps not through studying them letter by letter, but by configuration; that is, by retaining a picture of the total word instead of thinking of the component letters. At any rate, many first-grade children can write independently as many as 50 to 100 words by the end of the school year, and in the second grade they continue to learn many words through incidental means.

Even in situations in which the second-grade program includes regular spelling lessons based on a locally prescribed list or on a text-book, the chances are that, with the help of the teacher, second-grade children will also have their own list of words selected on the basis of current writing needs. One effective procedure is for each child to have a sturdy cardboard word box about a foot long and five inches wide. In it should be twenty-six stiff guide cards, each with a letter of the alphabet on a projection at the top. Then, as a useful word that a pupil wishes to master is met, the child can write the word on a piece of paper and file it alphabetically. Thereafter, he may consult his word box for any word he has placed there.

Teachers who are trying to determine a local list will do well to consult graded lists such as those presented by Fitzgerald or Hildreth. (See Bibliography at the end of this chapter.) Any word of current need that seems too hard or that the children do not need to master at the present time may be listed temporarily on the board or on a chart so that the children may copy the word when they need to write it. For those words that are likely to be generally useful, spelling les-sons may be planned.

When a prescribed spelling text is used in second grade, perhaps the best procedure is to consult the summary list that most spellers and spelling workbooks offer for review at the end of the book. From this list may be selected the words for which the pupils have immediate and frequent need. A check mark may be placed before each word that is selected and taught. Thus much of the year's spelling list may be covered. An individual pupil may also have a list of words that he compiles on the basis of his personal needs.

Children should, in general, learn the spelling of such words as they need to use frequently in their writing. From among the new words learned in connection with a group experience or current interest, the teacher and the children should select those key words that may be needed in writing a picture legend, a label, a notice, or a story. These words should be written on a chart and kept for the duration of the activity or interest so that the children may consult the list as need arises. For example, while interest persists in the trip to the train mentioned earlier in this book, the following words may be listed:

trip	sidetrack	steam	conductor
train	dining car	engine	porter
ready	sleeper	engineer	passenger

By no means should the children be expected to master the spelling of these words. Yet such a reference list instills in the child the idea that *there is a correct way to spell any word,* and it establishes the habit of finding out the correct spelling when he does not know it. The child should also be encouraged to ask the teacher for a correct spelling when he is doing original writing.

Handwriting

Skill in handwriting will condition the effectiveness of a child's written expression. Therefore, handwriting is a factor in the language arts program. It is not the function of this book to prescribe the procedures for the teaching of writing. Each system of writing instruction gives specific directions for teaching manuscript or cursive writing. It is necessary, however, for the teacher to recognize the fact that as long as a child must be completely absorbed in his efforts to form the letters —must concentrate on what his fingers are doing—he cannot concentrate on the ideas he has set out to express. When a child omits words from his sentences, when he omits letters from words that he really knows how to spell, when his sentences are barren and but vaguely connected in thought, then the teacher must consider whether having to make a tremendous effort to write is at least one source of his trouble. It is worth the time and effort to give extra attention to that child in the writing period or in special periods for individual instruction.

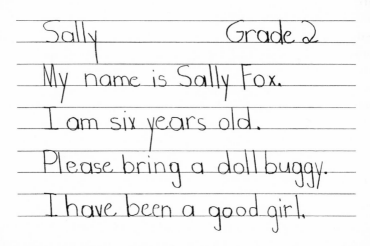

The approach of Christmas motivated Sally to write this appeal for a special gift. This is especially good writing and general arrangement for a young child in early second grade.

The teacher must be sure that the regular lessons and exercises in learning manuscript writing forms carry over into normal writing situations. Most lessons in manuscript writing are tied to reading, social studies, or other current classroom activities. The children have thought of a sentence or two that they wish to write. The teacher writes it on the board and the children copy it.

However, certain letters may be difficult to make, and specific practice on such letters may be desirable. Before the close of such a practice lesson in writing, it is well to ask each child to write a sentence telling something he wishes to say, or to dictate a sentence for him to write—perhaps a sentence about some interesting class experience of the day, or to let one of the children suggest an interesting sentence to write. Even at the risk of a misspelled word or an omitted period, it is desirable to have the child's writing effort carry over into the practical situation of using writing to express thought so that the act of writing may become almost automatic.

The Teacher as Secretary

FOR GROUP COMMUNICATION

Much of the written expression in kindergarten and the first grade and possibly in the early part of the second grade will be the cooperative work of the group, in which children suggest various sentences, the group judges and selects the one that is preferred, and the teacher writes the accepted sentence on the board. The daily news story, a report of the latest step in a class activity that will be part of a longer record of a unit as a whole, an announcement, a note or letter to mothers about a school party, various lists (names of pupil helpers, their duties, committee assignments, materials needed for a project)— these constitute most of the kinds of communication that the children will engage in. This type of writing activity is described fully in an earlier chapter. (Also note that schools using the language-experience approach have much of children's reading and writing in individual, not group, productions.)

FOR THE INDIVIDUAL CHILD

The teacher also records ideas for individual children. On some occasions, articles are brought by the children for a classroom exhibit, and each contributor may wish to make his own label. A child decides what he wants to write on his label, and the teacher writes it on a slip of paper for him to copy. On another occasion, a child may have drawn a picture and may then wish to compose a legend to explain it. Again, the teacher writes down what the child dictates so that he may copy his own legend.

After Christmas, each child in one second grade brought his favorite toy to school. The children were later asked if they would like to draw pictures of their toys. The response was enthusiastic, and crayons were immediately in evidence. As the children drew, the teacher moved among them. Inevitably some of them explained their pictures to her. Upon suggestion from the teacher, each child composed a story or legend for his picture. The teacher then wrote on a slip of paper the one or two sentences that the child dictated, and he later copied his story below the picture. At the suggestion of one child, the pictures were eventually made into a *Toyland Book,* which was a favorite in the classroom reading center.

An occasional imaginative child has a desire to make up stories or verse. He may have facility in writing down ideas for himself, but until a child has reached the stage of independent writing, the teacher acts as his secretary whenever he expresses a desire to record his creative production. She may reproduce the story or verse on a chart for the group to read or she may have it read orally to the group. The child often copies it and places it in a class book of stories and verse, or in his own book.

Preparation for Independent Writing

For children who do not develop writing skill with considerable ease, authorities in language instruction recommend definite steps in building up the fundamental skills involved in independent writing. These are: (1) copywork, (2) studied dictation, (3) unstudied dictation, (4) the unfinished story, and (5) independent writing. If possible, a series of lessons following these steps should be fitted in as part of a larger activity, such as the study of community helpers or of animal friends.

COPYWORK

Much of the copywork will follow pupils' individual or group dictation of stories, reports, announcements, or notes which have been written down by the teacher on a note pad or on the chalkboard. The teaching of the necessary skills of writing precedes the children's accomplishing any such copywork. The teacher calls their attention to the various elements of form such as placing the title, keeping a margin at the top and left side (possibly the right), indenting a paragraph (introduced about the time that they read from reading textbooks which are printed in true paragraph form), placing the parts of a note or letter, using capital letters and terminal punctuation in sentences, using such other capital letters and punctuation marks as the writing calls for, and spelling words correctly by consulting a personal word list or using any other spelling-help that the teacher provides. The children are instructed to copy by phrases rather than by the single

Children writing independently often ask for help in finding the words they need. The teacher circulates and gives children such words, pronouncing them in syllables as she writes.

word or by spelling out single words in a laborious way. The standard for all copywork is *perfection*—one hundred per cent accuracy. Almost without exception, children will at first copy what the "teacher-secretary" has written for them. Very bright children will soon develop considerable independence; slower-learning pupils will profit from lessons in studied dictation which are described below.

STUDIED DICTATION

After copywork has familiarized the group with manuscript form and with the common uses of capitalization and punctuation, the slow-learning children in mid-second grade will profit from lessons in studied dictation. The sentences, the note, the notice, or the story to be dictated should be studied under teacher direction. The teacher should list the words that children have not learned to spell, writing them on the board in the order of their appearance so that each word can be easily located by a child who needs to refer to the list. The teacher's dictation should follow a very specific technique, the steps being:

1. Read the entire selection (now concealed) while the children listen to recall the sentences in it.
2. Read the first sentence so that the children can visualize it and recall the capitalization and end punctuation.
3. Read the first thought phrase in the sentence (two to five words) while the children listen closely.
4. Have the children repeat the phrase that has just been read to offset their naturally short span of attention.
5. Have the children write what they have just repeated, looking at the board for the spelling of any difficult word.
6. Read the next phrase in the first sentence, have the children repeat it and write it.
7. Repeat steps 2–6 for each phrase within the sentence.
8. Follow steps 2–7 with each sentence.

As in copywork, the standard for dictation work is perfection, or as near one hundred per cent accuracy as possible. Each paper should be inspected by the teacher. Errors should be pointed out and discussed with each child, who then corrects them. By this procedure, children who do not easily master the mechanics of writing soon make real progress toward independent mastery of spelling, capitalization, and punctuation.

UNSTUDIED DICTATION

Some children soon become proficient in studied dictation, while others need much practice. The former group should proceed to independent writing, or, if this is still too advanced, to unstudied dictation as soon as they are ready for it; they should not wait for their slower-learning classmates.

In unstudied dictation, children dictate a cooperative story which the teacher writes on paper. The children do not see the story before they write. However, the teacher lists on the board, in the order of occurrence, any words whose spelling might prove troublesome. She should ask questions on items of form that will appear in the exercise, such as, "How do you write the name of a pet?" "How do you write the first word in a sentence?" In dictating, she should follow all the steps that are listed on page 134, as the children need this very detailed guidance for writing stories they have not previously read, discussed, and studied as to form.

THE UNFINISHED STORY

In an unfinished story, the beginning of a simple story is copied from the board or from a chart, or written from dictation. The teacher then suggests that the children imagine how the story might end and write the ending in their own words. The story should be of such character that the outcome may readily be sensed and may be expressed in one or two sentences. Specimens of unfinished stories follow.

The teacher begins in this manner: "Here is the beginning of a story. Let's read it. Then you may finish the story in your own way."

A Happy Surprise

David wanted a new pet. His black and white puppy had run away. It never came back. One morning David heard a sound outside the door. It was a soft little sound. . . .

Fun at Home

Would Saturday never come? Dennis and Rickie could hardly wait. They were going to the zoo to see the new baby polar bears. But it was raining Saturday! Then Mother planned a nice surprise. . . .

A variation of the unfinished story is changing the ending of a story in the reader. Here, in discussing the story, the teacher concludes by having a child or two tell a different ending. Then, in language period, the class works together to write a cooperative statement of the first part of this same story. Each child copies this before writing an ending that he has thought up for himself.

Often, before completing an unfinished story or writing a changed ending, the children are asked to suggest words they need but cannot spell. These the teacher puts on the chalkboard for ready reference. Any other words may be handled in one of these ways: (1) The child keeps a piece of scrap paper at the side. On this he tries out the spelling of an unfamiliar word. If it looks right, he includes it in the story. (2) He writes as much of the word as he believes himself to know and proceeds with his writing so as to preserve the thread of his thinking. Later he finds out how to complete the word. (3) He may leave a blank, and continue putting down his ideas. He can ascertain the correct spelling later. (4) The teacher moves among the pupils and writes a requested word on a child's bit of scrap paper.

Independent Writing

As soon as the more proficient children demonstrate ability to write down their ideas for themselves, they should be encouraged to do so. Any words they cannot spell may be dealt with in one of the ways suggested in the preceding paragraph.

PROCEDURES

In these first stages of independent writing, the children should use a procedure advisable throughout their school years—the practice of making a first draft wherein their primary concern is with getting their ideas on paper while these are fresh and enthusiasm is high. In writing this first draft, a child should first think through what he wishes to say —points in his story, the order for relating ideas, interesting words to use. Then he should write quite rapidly without pondering about spelling, punctuation, and similar mechanics. Afterward—possibly the next day—he will read through what he has written, check on possible improvements in choice of words and organization of ideas, and correct his spelling, capitalization, punctuation, and manuscript form (for example, indentation, margins, and placement of title). Using this first draft, he will cross out and write in substitutions to put his story in as satisfactory shape as possible. Then only will he make the final draft which his teacher and classmates may read and view on the bulletin board or perhaps only hear. A child who learns to make a rough draft with his story the main concern, who makes improvements on it afterward, and then copies it, has learned a practice that will do much toward guaranteeing effectiveness in writing all his life.

STANDARDS OF ATTAINMENT

By the end of the second grade, all the children should have gained some degree of ability to write independently, though all children may not have attained the same standard as to quality of content. In their independent writing, however, they should have established the following habits as to manuscript form and as to the mechanics of writing:

1. Place the correct heading at the top of the page in the right position, capitalizing correctly.
2. Keep a fairly even left margin about an inch wide.
3. Begin the first word in each sentence with a capital letter.
4. Capitalize the word *I*.
5. Place a period at the end of a statement.
6. Place a question mark at the end of a question.
7. Use capital letters for names of persons and pets.

Children should also be habitually neat in the final drafts of their written work and careful of their spelling. If the paragraph form is taught, indention will eventually become almost automatic.

Selected References

SPELLING

BENTHUL, HERMAN F., *et al.* *Spell Correctly.* Morristown, New Jersey: Silver Burdett Co., 1965.

CARLSON, G. R. "So They Can't Spell," *Education,* 79, December, 1958, pp. 219–23.

DAWSON, MILDRED and DINGEE, FRIEDA. *Children Learn the Language Arts.* Minneapolis: Burgess Publishing Co., 1960.

FITZGERALD, JAMES A. *A Basic Life Spelling Vocabulary.* Milwaukee: The Bruce Publishing Co., 1951.

————. "The Selection of Vocabulary for Basic Spelling Instruction," *Education,* 76, January, 1956.

FURNESS, ETHEL. *Spelling for the Millions.* New York: Appleton-Century-Crofts, Inc., 1964.

GROFF, PATRICK. "Visual and Auditory Perception Training and Spelling Achievement," *Elementary English,* February, 1965.

HANNA, PAUL. "Spelling and Communication Theory," *Elementary School Journal,* 1963.

HILDRETH, GERTRUDE. *Teaching Spelling.* New York: Henry Holt and Co., 1956.

MASON, GEOFFREY P. "Word Discrimination and Spelling," *Journal of Educational Research,* 50, April, 1957.

RICHMOND, A. E. "Children's Spelling Needs and the Implications of Research," *Journal of Experimental Education,* 29, September, 1960.

RUSSELL, DAVID H. *Characteristics of Good and Poor Spellers.* New York: Bureau of Publications, Teachers College, Columbia University, 1937.

STRICKLAND, RUTH. "Utilizing Spelling Research," *Childhood Education,* 32, October, 1955.

ZEDLER, EMPRESS Y. "Effect of Phonic Training on Speech Sound Discrimination and Spelling Performance," *Journal of Speech and Hearing Disorders,* June, 1956.

SENTENCES AND PARAGRAPHS

COMMISSION ON THE ENGLISH CURRICULUM. *Language Arts for Today's Children,* Chapter 8. New York: Appleton-Century-Crofts, Inc., 1954.

ANDERSON, PAUL S. *Language Skills in Elementary Education,* Chapters 5 and 8. New York: The Macmillan Co., 1964.

DAWSON, MILDRED and DINGEE, FRIEDA. *Children Learn the Language Arts,* pp. 93–95. Minneapolis: Burgess Publishing Co., 1959.

DAWSON, MILDRED, *et al.* *Guiding Language Learning,* Chapter 14. New York: Harcourt, Brace & World, Inc., 1963.

GREENE, HARRY A. and PETTY, WALTER T. *Developing Language Skills in the Elementary School,* Chapters 6 and 12. Boston: Allyn & Bacon, Inc., 1959.

SHANE, HAROLD, *et al. Improving Language Arts Instruction in the Elementary School,* pp. 413–23. Columbus, Ohio: Charles Merrill Books, Inc., 1962.

STRICKLAND, RUTH G. *Language Arts in the Elementary School,* Chapter 12. Boston: D. C. Heath & Co., 1957.

Simulated telephone booths equipped with telephones give the teacher an especially good opportunity to observe individual speech habits, as children enjoy the drama of telephone conversation, and talk spontaneously.

7
Improvement
of Language

TEACHERS IN the kindergarten-primary grades know full well that the correct usage of words is of minor importance in children's language in comparison with the vital significance of their having wide interests and rich experiences that lead to fluency and spontaneity of verbal expression. Making sure that children have ideas to express and a desire to express them interestingly and effectively are the more important ends to be sought in developing the language arts program for the younger school children.

It is possible, however, for a teacher to help her pupils to develop habits of correct speech and to eliminate much of the incorrect usage without impairing spontaneity or destroying the social values of communication. There are a few really gross errors in word usage that she should strive to eliminate. As a classroom teacher, she should be able to recognize the simpler speech difficulties and know how to remove them.

Investigations in the field of language have demonstrated that few errors in speech and in word usage are common to an entire group. Errors are highly individualized, and the teacher will have to plan much small-group and individual instruction.

Survey of Group Habits of Word Usage

A prerequisite of work in word usage is a careful survey of the usage habits of the group. It will be discovered that some children make al-

most no errors of the flagrant type, thus reflecting a home environment
in which they hear fairly good language. There is the possibility, however, that most of the children will enunciate a few sounds improperly
or use some grossly incorrect word forms common to the community.
When this is the case, the teacher should list those errors for stress.

In general, the survey becomes a task of observing individual habits
of expression as children talk spontaneously. Probably not all errors
made by the children can be eliminated, but a few should be listed for
special stress. The following lists suggest those errors from which the
teacher may select.

I. Speech faults
    Baby talk
    Lisping
    Faulty sounding of **l, sh, s, r, z, th,** and **wh**

II. Word usage
    Forms that are not words, or are mispronunciations; as,

"hain't"	"growed"	"yourn"
"brung"	"knowed"	"youse"
"clumb"	"hisn"	"hisself"
"bust"	"ourn"	"theirselves"

    The impolite habit of mentioning oneself first; as,
            "I and Father" went.
            Please help "me and Jim."

    Some flagrant errors with verbs in frequent use; as,
        "I done it."   "He come late yesterday."
        "I seen it."   "I run home last night."
            "He has went."

    Incorrect expressions; as,
            "them books"   "this here clay"
            "that there picture"

Part I above is especially important in the first grade, whereas attention to items in Part II should be handled incidentally and individu-
ally, even in the second grade. Because children vary so greatly with
respect to the speech faults listed in Part I, it is usually necessary to
deal with individual children in trying to eliminate these faults. No
teacher should attempt to work on all the errors listed. The attempt to

work on many errors leads to inhibitions and causes the teacher to neglect the more important expressional activities.

The Program in Speech

The improvement of speech is a very important phase of the language arts program. While the specialist in speech is the only one qualified to treat an occasional serious speech defect in a child, the classroom teacher can do much to improve the more or less faulty speech of all children in the group. The program in speech should be directed toward (1) voice quality, (2) enunciation, (3) pronunciation, and (4) expression or intonation to convey meaning.

A PLANNED AND CONSISTENT PROGRAM

In general, children in the kindergarten-primary grades need a planned and consistent course of training in speech. They still retain many of the careless habits of speech picked up (through imitation) in the preschool years. In fact, in many homes, parents and older children actually enjoy the "baby talk" and the incorrect pronunciation of letter sounds in the speech of the younger child in the home, and thus promote persistence of faulty articulation into the school years.

Some of these irregularities of speech are due to incorrect use of the organs of speech, some to immaturity, some to faulty hearing, some to lack of attentive listening, and some to mere ignorance of correct letter sounds. The program of speech correction must therefore be directed along several lines.

Since instruction in speech is such an important aspect of the language arts program, affecting both reading and expression, many second-grade teachers find it necessary to have a set of supplementary speech readers for use by the children who need correction. The use of a well-planned text of this type helps the teacher to promote a logical and consistent—in truth, a correct—program for the improvement of speech within her group.

VOICE QUALITY

Children unconsciously imitate adults—a fact that sometimes leads to desirable and often to undesirable practices on the part of children.

It is therefore important that the teacher's voice and speech be such as to yield desirable results whenever her group imitates her.

The teacher's voice should be well-rounded (not thin), moderately pitched (especially not too high), of moderate volume (not loud), melodious or well-modulated (not flat or monotonous), pleasing (not harsh or shrill), and lively (not drawling or languid). Children who work with a teacher having a pleasing, well-modulated voice and a stimulating, alert, interested manner of speaking are likely to speak in similar tones. If the teacher enunciates distinctly so that she need not raise her voice to make children hear and understand her words, the children unconsciously acquire similar clarity of enunciation. Children may be helped to acquire flexible, expressive voices if they have many opportunities to repeat verse with contrasting ideas and to read aloud conversation that reflects varying emotions such as surprise, joy, and fear. Choral reading is also an aid to voice improvement.

Structural characteristics of the vocal chambers largely determine the fundamental tonal qualities of the voice. However, a high-pitched, nasal, or monotonous voice is often imitative or merely a matter of habit; it can usually be changed through intelligent training. A few pupils may need individual attention if their voice placement is far back in the throat, too high in the head, or forward in the nasal passages.

ENUNCIATION

Young children often speak indistinctly because they do not use their lips, teeth (or jaws), and tongue actively. The teacher may sometimes demonstrate the use of these organs of speech by pronouncing some vowels and consonants with somewhat exaggerated use of lips, teeth, and tongue.

Demonstrations might well proceed in the following order. While lips, teeth, and tongue perform a function in making all letter sounds, there are certain consonants that use one or the other conspicuously, as indicated:

> Lips: **b f m p** v w y
> Teeth (Jaws) **c d f g h j k s t v z**
> Tongue: **d l n s x z**

Practice in pronouncing words beginning and ending with these consonants will help children to use their lips, teeth, and tongue effectively. Pairs of words like the following may be written on a chart or the board, pronounced by the teacher with emphasis on beginning and ending sounds and with slightly exaggerated movement of lips, jaws, and tongue, and then repeated by the children:

bat —rub	me —am	kite—lick
funny—gruff	want—now	like —will
do —red	to —not	nice—soon

Enunciation of internal consonant sounds should be practiced by repeating such words as:

rubber	sudden	gully	wither	matter
ribbon	hidden	silly	mother	bitter
labor	rider	gaily	father	later

In pronouncing such words, the children may slightly exaggerate the use of lips, teeth, and tongue in producing beginning, internal, and final consonant sounds. The exaggeration provides a kind of exercise for limbering up the muscles of lips, tongue, and jaw and making them more flexible and active. Such demonstration and practice will be sufficient for the majority of the group. The "lazy" speaker—a child who enunciates letters or words with scarcely a visible movement of lips, teeth, and tongue—will need intensive individual training in the enunciation of consonants.

Attention should also be given to the placement of vowel sounds. The child can readily feel that these sounds arise from the back of the mouth cavity, though the different vowel sounds and the different sounds of a single vowel will require different manipulation of teeth and lips. The following more common sounds of each vowel should be demonstrated by the teacher to show clearly how the sound is placed:

ā (āble)	ē (ēven)	ī (īce)	ō (ōld)	ū (ūse)
ă (ăt)	ĕ (ĕnd)	ĭ (ĭt)	ŏ (ŏdd)	ŭ (ŭp)
ä (ärm)				

The diacritical markings need not be taught. It is better to list words like the following for the children to read and pronounce:

	Sounds of a			*Sounds of e*	
able	at	arm	eat	end
ate	am	art	feel	echo
take	fan	farm	beet	leg

	Sounds of i		*Sounds of o*		*Sounds of u*	
ice	it	old	odd	use	up
nice	tin	over	ox	June	uncle
fine	sink	cold	fox	music	sun

The main stress in the work with enunciation, however, will have to do with the pronunciation of words in sentences. Nonsense sentences containing a number of words beginning or ending with the same marked letter sounds are also helpful with "lazy" speakers. Sentences like the following may be written on the board and used for oral practice:

Fred found four fine files.
Tell Tony to take two turns.
Let Scott put that cat out.

The teacher may also make good use of nursery rhymes. The following are titles of rhymes that feature sounds that the children may need to practice:

d	Diddle, Diddle, Dumpling
s	Swan, Swan, over the Sea
w	Wee Willie Winkie
m	One Misty, Moisty Morning
p	Peter, Peter, Pumpkin Eater
g	Goosey, Goosey, Gander

Further attention to the enunciation of words in normal sentences should be a part of regular reading lessons.

PRONUNCIATION

The general practice described in the preceding section may not correct the mispronunciation of certain letters that persists with individual children. The teacher may easily detect such children in the ordinary work in reading. There may be an occasional child who cannot produce correctly the sound of *r*, or *l*, or *w*. Such a child needs individual instruction as to the correct sound of the letter and as to the correct placement and use of speech organs to produce the correct letter sound.

Some young children have difficulty in pronouncing consonant blends such as *br*, *cr*, *dr*, *fr*, *gr*, *pr*, and *tr*, *sw* and *tw*, *bl*, *cl*, *pl* and *sl*, and digraphs like *wh* and *th*. These children may require special instruction and practice along the lines suggested for remedial work on individual letter sounds.

The mispronunciation of certain consonant combinations may be due to a failure to sense letter values, or to the careless disregard of the sound value of one letter. Among such combinations are initial *wh* and final *ng*. Instruction and practice with lists of words like the following are helpful in correcting these faults:

wh			ng	
white	when	whale	ring	doing
while	what	whip	sing	being
where	why	whack	bring	flying
which	wheat	whine	wing	going

Such catch-sayings as "Always make *ing* rhyme with *ring*" and "Start to whistle when you say *white*" are helpful reminders.

Other initial combinations that may need attention are *ch*, *sh*, and *th* (both sounds). Final combinations *sh*, *th*, *tch*, and *est* may also need stress. Repeating nonsense sentences embodying such letter combinations will be helpful.

The teacher should watch for other mispronunciations common

among the children and list them for correction as a phase of the speech program. Some of the more frequent errors concern the following words:

wish (not "woosh" or "wisht")   help (not "hep")
wash (not "warsh")   ask (not "ast")
any (not "inny")   hold (not "holt")
men (not "min")   heard (not "heerd")
best (not "bes")   burst (not "bust")

The child who mispronounces such words should not be made self-conscious by untactful correction. A group or an individual needing special attention should be taken aside while the rest of the children are otherwise engaged and given special corrective instruction through pleasurable activities such as group speaking or speech games.

It is always best to conduct the speech lessons apart from those periods in which spontaneous oral expression is the goal. During a period of the latter type, the teacher may unobtrusively observe speech needs on the part of the individual and the group and make them the basis of special speech lessons. The use of a supplementary speech text is one good means of keeping speech instruction apart from other oral-expression periods.

VOICE MODULATION

Training in modulation of the voice to bring out the meaning of words and phrases within a sentence, as well as the sentence as a whole, is best handled in the reading period. All good teachers of reading now realize that "word calling" is not reading. Children are reminded to "read the sentence as you would say it yourself" or "read it as you think Betty said it."

Children's spontaneous speech is seldom monotonous or singsong. In fact, from babyhood, a child will generally make his tone of voice and verbal intonations reflect his emotion and his meaning. It is only when he is placed in a formal speech situation—perhaps in an unduly laborious oral reading class where he must struggle to recognize words —that he begins to utter words and sentences in a monotonous and lifeless manner. When the language periods are characterized by a freedom and a social atmosphere that invite spontaneous expression, children are likely to speak expressively. Similarly, when the reading period is a period of pleasurable experience during which the child enjoys the thought of what he reads and senses it as the interesting expression of others (rather than a testing period in which the teacher seeks to discover how many words he knows), the child will generally read in a fluent and meaningful fashion.

Dramatic reading is one type of exercise calling for special emphasis on expression. For such reading, the teacher asks different children to take the parts of the various characters in the story, and she herself (or other children) reads the parts that carry the story continuity. When children read the parts of the characters, they are advised to "show how the person felt" and to "say it as you think Bob must have said it," thus attaining the desired end of reading with expression.

Dramatization of favorite stories, in which the children recall the dialogue or compose their own speeches, is another means of developing the habit of showing meaning and emotion through the use of the voice. If some children are slow in developing the desired ability in expression, either through timidity or through lack of imagination, their tendency to imitate the expression of their abler classmates will in time override their deficiencies if there is plenty of spontaneous dramatization.

LISTENING TO ORAL READING

Listening to stories and poems read by the teacher is another influence toward the improvement of expression—provided, of course, that *the teacher herself reads well.* A teacher who wishes to bring to her group the fullest enjoyment of literature, as well as the concomitant value of improvement of voice and expression, must practice in reading aloud and even rehearse until voice, enunciation, pronunciation, and expression are clear, lively, and expressive.

Chapter 4 of this book discusses at length the function of the teacher in reading and telling stories and in reading poems. The bibliography at the close of that chapter lists books on the art of storytelling, as well as anthologies of stories and poems that will serve as sources of appropriate materials for reading aloud. Within the chapter are lists of poems that the teacher may well read aloud.

Methods of Attack on Word Usage

When it is apparent that a given error in word usage persists with an individual or a group, corrective measures should be concentrated upon it. The accepted steps of procedure are:

1. The children look at the correct form on the board or on a chart. (*eye training*)
2. The children listen to the teacher's repetition of the correct form. (*ear training*)
3. They say the form aloud correctly. (*ear and speech training*)
4. They read the form correctly in a sentence, or repeat the sentence after the teacher. (*habit forming*)

It is helpful to have the forms for special stress written on charts that may be taken from files and used as needs demand. The following charts were used by one teacher in a campaign against "ain't" and "hain't."

am not	**isn't**
I am not ready.	Joe isn't here.
I am not late.	Isn't that a robin?
I am not hungry.	Anne isn't coming.
I am not tired.	Isn't it cold today?
aren't	**haven't**
The books aren't here.	Haven't you a pencil?
Aren't you going?	We haven't voted yet.
You aren't my partner.	Haven't you seen Sue?
Aren't we invited?	I haven't any crayons.

Necessarily, the sentences for such charts should be chosen from those frequently used by the children, and the words must be selected from the reading vocabulary. Since children learn their speech habits through imitation of forms and expressions that they hear, *ear training* is an important factor in developing habits of correct usage. With any child or any group requiring special practice, the proper method is to place the chart showing correct form before the child, have him read it aloud, and then have him make up sentences using the correct forms. The latter should be inspired by skillful questioning.

The preferred method of instruction in correct usage, then, follows these principles:

1. Individualize the instruction.
2. Concentrate on a very few forms.
3. Present the correct form to eye and ear.
4. Have children repeat the correct form aloud in sentences, some of which are composed by the child.
5. Feature the correct form in many reading charts.

An alert teacher will find frequent opportunities for a few seconds of practice. At the beginning of a drawing period, when all are at attention, she may briefly ask, "*Have you* a red crayon, Jill?" The child should reply, "Yes, *I have* a red crayon" (not "I've got").

In a moment of free time, the teacher may ask, "Who *ate* the Little Bear's porridge, Joe?" Joe should reply, "Goldilocks *ate* the Little Bear's porridge."

SPIRIT OF CORRECTION

Sometimes correction may be given at the time that an error is made, provided that the child is not interrupted in his flow of thought and that he is not embarrassed. For example, Johnny may remark, "Father done the dishes for Mother last night." Upon the conclusion of this remark, the teacher may quietly say, "Your father *did* the dishes. Who *did* them the night before?" in the hope that the child will seize upon the correct form *did* from her own purposeful use of it. If Johnny is a shy child, she may wait until she can speak to him alone. However, if he is a well-adjusted child who can take suggestions without embarrassment, she may unobtrusively and privately suggest at once, "Say 'Father *did* the dishes,' Johnny," in a casual and friendly manner. On the whole, it is preferable that the teacher find frequent occasion to use the correct form of words that the children use improperly. As she does so, the right word will begin to *sound right* to the children, and they will begin unconsciously to imitate her.

Language Games

In general, so-called language games are not highly successful in habituating correct usage. However, with a few children who are slow to grasp a correct form (which has previously been properly developed) and who need to hear it repeated frequently, language games may be tried.

The primary consideration in selecting and introducing a game is that the game itself be such that attention does not center on the game activity but that concentration upon *correct usage* is paramount—that the children be ready to center upon *language* as the major interest. When lack of interest in a game is apparent, it should be stopped immediately. In any event, such a game should not be prolonged more than a few minutes.

The following games are examples of what may be done:

HIDING THE BALL
(To eliminate "has got" and "ain't")

Jack is chosen to leave the room. During his absence, Gladys, the leader, gives a ball to Ralph, who holds his hands behind him, thus hiding the ball. The rest of the children also place their hands behind them.

Gladys calls Jack to return to the room. Then she asks, "Jack, who *has* the ball?"

> JACK (*looking at Mary*). Is it Mary?
>
> GLADYS. No, it *isn't* Mary.
>
> JACK. Is it Dick?
>
> GLADYS. No, it *isn't* Dick.
>
> JACK. Is it Ralph?
>
> GLADYS. Yes, it is Ralph.

Ralph then leaves the room, and the game proceeds.

Language games are not generally used to develop correct word usage, but a word game may occasionally be used for drill after the skill has been developed. Here the child fishes for every word he recognizes and can pronounce.

Dyer Street Elementary School, Sylmar, California

TAKE A PEEP
(Practice with *I saw*)

Under a cover on a table or desk, the teacher has concealed a number of small common objects. She then asks, "Anne, will you take a quick peep and tell us one thing that you *saw?*

Anne walks to the table, lifts the cover slightly, and notices one object.

TEACHER. What did you see, Anne?

ANNE. I *saw* a watch.

TEACHER. Bob, take a peep and look for something else.

(*Bob steps forward and looks under the cover.*)

TEACHER. Bob, what did you see?

BOB. I *saw* a knife.

Other children take their turns in similar manner.

At another time the game may be varied by having the children "take a peep" through a window.

COLORS
(Practice with *isn't*)

One child, Tom, is told to think of a color. The game proceeds as follows:

TOM. I am thinking of a color.

EDNA. Is it the color of Mary's dress?

TOM. No, it *isn't* red.

GRACE. Is it the color of this crayon?

TOM. No, it *isn't* green.

GEORGE. Is it the color of the sky?

This is the right color, *blue,* and instead of answering, Tom claps his hands. The one who guessed the color now chooses a color, and the game goes on.

WHO DID IT?
(Practice with *did*)

A leader is appointed, and the leader selects a player who is "It." The player closes his eyes. The leader points to a child, and that child immediately claps his hands softly.

The player then opens his eyes, and the leader says, "Somebody clapped. Who did it?"

The player replies, "I think ___?___ *did* it."

If this is the correct guess, the child named says, "Yes, I *did* it," and changes places with the player. The game then begins again.

If a wrong guess is made, the child named shakes his head but says nothing. The leader then asks the same question again. If the player does not guess after making three trials, a new player is appointed and the game proceeds.

Play the game rapidly, and change the leader after a while.

Anyone who uses the word *done* instead of *did* must play "echo." That is, another child gives the answer correctly, and the one who missed must echo it.

Similar games can be devised at the discretion of the teacher for the correction of any gross errors that a few children in her group make. The game should be simple in execution, as are the ones above; the responses should stress a particular correct usage; and the game should be pursued but a few minutes and with the few children who really need the practice. Otherwise, interest will lag and the game be ineffective in producing desired results.

Selected References

CORRECT USAGE

DAWSON, MILDRED A., *et al.* *Guiding Language Learning*, Chapter 29. New York: Harcourt, Brace & World, Inc., 1963.

POOLEY, ROBERT. *Teaching English Usage.* New York: Appleton-Century-Crofts, Inc.

THE TEACHING OF SPEECH

BARNES, HARRY GRINNELL. *Speech Handbook.* 2nd ed. Englewood Cliffs, New Jersey: Prentice-Hall, Inc., 1959.

BEASLEY, J. *Show Talk.* New York: Bureau of Publications, Teachers College, Columbia University, 1956.

BRYNGELSON, BRYNA and MIKALSON, ELAINE. *Speech Correction Through Listening.* Chicago: Scott, Foresman and Co., 1959.

CARRELL, JAMES. *Phonetics: Theory and Application.* New York: McGraw-Hill Book Co., Inc., 1959.

FLETCHER, HARVEY. *Speech and Hearing in Communication.* New York: D. Van Nostrand Co., Inc., 1953.

JONES, MORRIS VAL. *Speech Correction at Home.* Springfield, Illinois: Charles C Thomas, Publisher, 1957.

PIERCE, JOHN ROBINSON. *Man's World of Sound.* New York: Doubleday & Co., Inc., 1958.

SCHOOLFIELD, LUCILLE. *Better Speech, Better Reading, A Practice Book.* Revised ed. Magnolia, Massachusetts: Expression Co., Publishers, 1957.

SCHREIBER, FLORA RHETA. *Your Child's Speech.* New York: G. P. Putnam's Sons, 1956.

SCOTT, LOUISE and THOMPSON, J. *Speech Ways.* St. Louis: Webster Publishing Co., 1955.

TEMPLIN, MILDRED. *Certain Language Skills in Children.* Minneapolis: University of Minnesota Press, 1957.

URIS, DOROTHY. *Everybody's Book of Better Speaking.* New York: David McKay Co., Inc., 1960.

VON HESSE, ELIZABETH. *So to Speak.* Philadelphia: J. B. Lippincott Co., 1959.

Index